THE SUN

Michael E. Picray

www.av2books.com

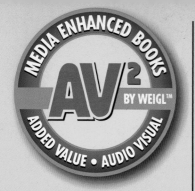

AV² provides enriched content that supplements and complements this book. Weigl's AV² books strive to create inspired learning and engage young minds in a total learning experience.

Your AV² Media Enhanced books come alive with...

Audio
Listen to sections of the book read aloud.

Key Words
Study vocabulary, and complete a matching word activity.

Video
Watch informative video clips.

Quizzes
Test your knowledge.

Go to **www.av2books.com**, and enter this book's unique code.

Embedded Weblinks
Gain additional information for research.

Slide Show
View images and captions, and prepare a presentation.

BOOK CODE

U 6 2 6 1 4 5

Try This!
Complete activities and hands-on experiments.

... and much, much more!

AV² by Weigl brings you media enhanced books that support active learning.

Published by AV² by Weigl
350 5th Avenue, 59th Floor
New York, NY 10118
Website: www.av2books.com   www.weigl.com

Library of Congress Control Number: 2012941989
ISBN 978-1-61913-097-5 (hard cover)
ISBN 978-1-61913-544-4 (soft cover)

Printed in the United States of America in North Mankato, Minnesota
1 2 3 4 5 6 7 8 9   16 15 14 13 12

062012
WEP170512

Editor Aaron Carr
Design Ken Clarke

Every reasonable effort has been made to trace ownership and to obtain permission to reprint copyright material. The publishers would be pleased to have any errors or omissions brought to their attention so that they may be corrected in subsequent printings.

Weigl acknowledges Getty Images as its primary image supplier for this title.

CONTENTS

Most of the energy on Earth comes from the Sun. Even **fossil fuels**, such as coal and oil, come from plants that trapped the Sun's energy millions of years ago. Today, humans can use energy from the Sun directly in the form of solar power. Solar power can be collected as heat, or it can be turned directly into electricity with solar panels. Solar power is a form of energy that has a much lower impact on the environment than fossil fuels.

Studying the Sun

The star that is nearest to Earth shines down on people every day.
This star is the Sun. It is the brightest object visible from Earth.
The Sun provides Earth with light and heat. There would not be
life on Earth without the Sun's energy.

In ancient times, people believed that the Sun was a life-giving
force. They knew that this glowing object in the sky gave life to
plants, animals, and humans.

■ The Sun is the largest object in the solar system. It is about 864,000 miles (1.4 million kilometers)
wide. The Sun could fit the planet Earth across its diameter 109 times.

What Is the Sun?

The Sun is a large ball of glowing gas. **Hydrogen** is the main gas that forms the Sun. The temperature of the Sun's surface is about 10,000° Fahrenheit (5,538°Celsius). It is even hotter above and below the surface of the Sun. The Sun's **core** is about 27 million°F (15 million°C).

Stars that formed just after the universe began are called first-generation stars. Second-generation stars formed from the material left behind by first-generation stars. The Sun is a second-generation star.

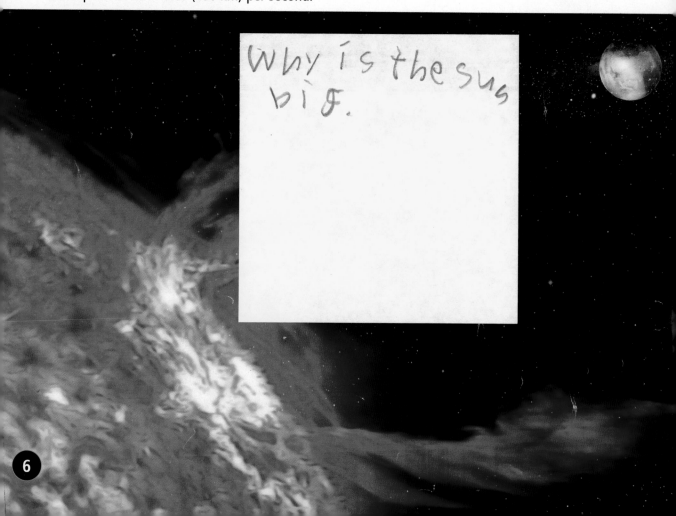

The Sun releases energy as a solar wind. This energy travels through the solar system at a speed of 280 miles (450 km) per second.

LAYERS OF THE SUN

1 Corona
The corona is much hotter than any area of the Sun except its core. Some scientists think that the Sun's intense electrical activity may be responsible for this.

2 Chromosphere
This is a thick layer around the outer edge of the Sun. It can only be seen during an eclipse, when the moon blocks most of the Sun's surface from view.

3 Photosphere
The photosphere is the part of the Sun that produces the light people see every day. **Sunspots** also occur on this layer.

4 Convection Zone
This area of the Sun is like a giant storm. Hot pockets of solar gas rise up and fall back toward the core as they cool.

5 Radiative Zone
In this zone, **radiation** from the Sun's core bounces back and forth, losing energy. Eventually, this radiation is released as light.

6 Core
This is the area of the Sun that produces energy. The Sun's strong **gravity** crushes hydrogen together until it becomes helium. This reaction produces the Sun's heat and light.

I think the Sun is not the same as earth inside

Stories of the Sun

In ancient times, many people admired the Sun because it gave life. People also feared the Sun for its extreme heat. Other ancient peoples prayed to the Sun, believing it to be a powerful god. The ancient Norse and Egyptian people were just two of the many groups who believed that the Sun was a god.

The Norse people called the Sun Sol. They believed that the Sun was a goddess. Sol was chased across the sky every day by a wolf named Skoll.

The Egyptians called their Sun god Ra. He was an important god to the Egyptians. Ra was often shown as having a human body and a hawk's head, with the orb of the Sun floating above it. He was said to travel through the sky every day in a sailing craft.

Ancient Egyptians believed Ra called all forms of life into being by calling them by their secret names.

The Fall of Icarus

A Greek **myth** tells about a boy named Icarus. Icarus and his father, Daedalus were in an island prison. To escape, Daedalus made wings of wax and feathers for himself and his son. Icarus and Daedalus used these wings to fly away from the island. Daedalus warned Icarus not to fly too close to the Sun. Icarus did not listen to the warning. The Sun's heat melted the wax, and his wings came apart. Icarus fell to his death.

The story of Icarus and Daedalus has been told many times throughout the centuries, in poems, stories, paintings, and sculptures.

Seasons and the Sun

Earth **orbits** the Sun. It takes 365.25 days, or one year, for Earth to complete one orbit. Over the course of this orbit, Earth tilts toward and away from the Sun. The Earth spins like a top while it orbits the Sun. The Sun shines on different parts of the Earth throughout the year. North America tilts towards the Sun in summer. This is why summer is warm. North America tilts away from the Sun in winter. This is why winter is the coldest season.

EARTH'S ROTATION AROUND THE SUN

Earth's tilt is what causes the days to be longer during summer and shorter during winter. For people in the northern half of Earth, or northern hemisphere, the Sun shines at a more direct angle. During winter, the Sun shines at an extreme angle.

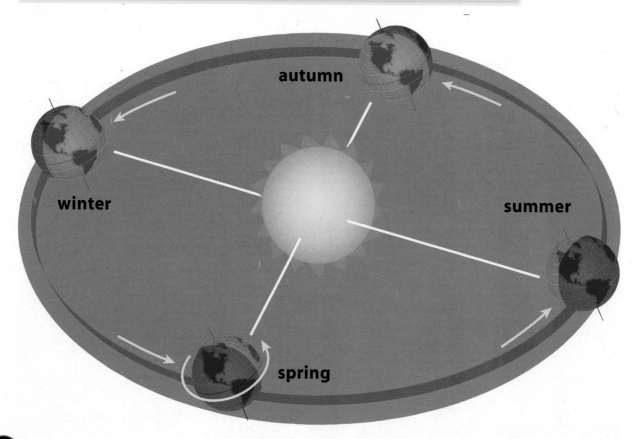

autumn

winter

summer

spring

Solar Energy

The Sun gives off energy in the form of light. This is called solar energy. For thousands of years, people have used the Sun's energy to heat their homes and even to cook. Today, people have invented a new way to use the Sun's energy. Sunlight is turned into electricity using solar panels.

Scientists and engineers have come up with creative ways to use solar power. Deserts get more sunlight than any other place on Earth. Solar panel arrays in deserts across the United States and northern Africa could make as much power as many smaller power plants. Scientists have also thought of using **satellites** to collect solar energy from space. Solar energy may one day become Earth's main energy source.

■ Scientists estimate that enough solar energy falls on a 100-square-mile (260-square-kilometer) section of the United States to power the whole country.

The Solar System

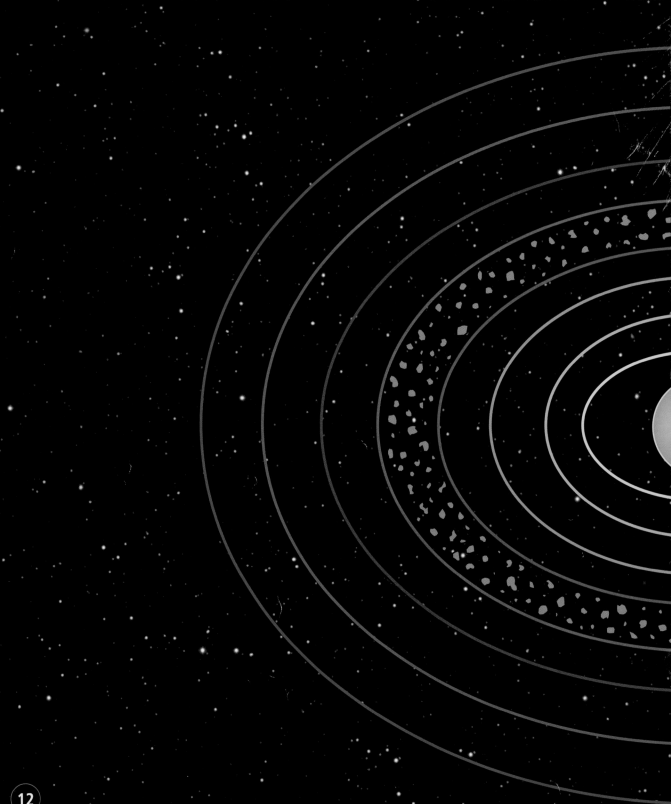

WHAT HAVE YOU LEARNED ABOUT THE SOLAR SYSTEM?

This map shows the planets and other features of the solar system. Use this map, and research in the library and online, to answer these questions.

1. What is the asteroid belt? Where is it located?
2. What is a gas giant? Which planets are gas giants?

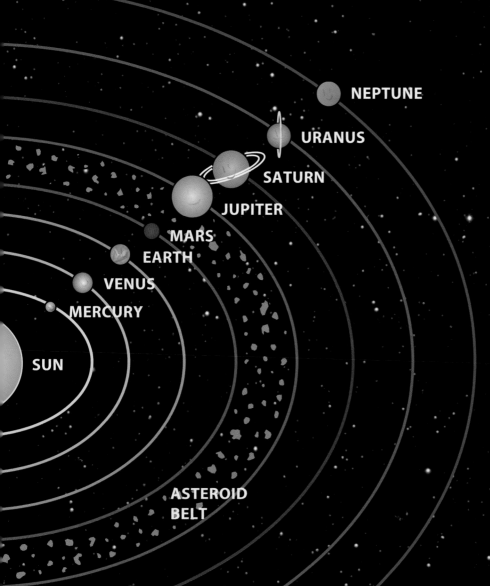

NEPTUNE

URANUS

SATURN

JUPITER

MARS

EARTH

VENUS

MERCURY

SUN

ASTEROID BELT

The Sun in Nature

All of the world's food requires the Sun's energy to grow. Green plants use the light energy from the Sun to make their food. This process is called photosynthesis. Animals and humans eat plants. They take in the Sun's energy that is stored inside. The Sun's energy also creates weather by heating the air. Wind and storms are caused by warm and cold air moving around each other. Earth would not have wind or rain without the Sun.

A Guiding Light

Humans have used the Sun as a guide for thousands of years. Ancient peoples would use the position of the Sun in the sky to steer their ships. Some animals also use the Sun as a guide.

In the fall, monarch butterflies fly from cool areas to warm areas. They use the Sun as a **compass** when they travel. The location of the Sun in the sky directs their **migration**. Monarch butterflies migrate more than 2,000 miles (3,219 km). These butterflies spend the winter in places such as Mexico and California. In the summer, they can move as far north as Canada and New England.

The monarch butterfly has the longest migration of any animal in North America.

Sun Science

The Sun is an important object of scientific study. Scientists are always trying to learn more about the closest star to Earth. They use satellites, space probes, and **telescopes** to study the Sun. Scientists can also study the Sun from the International Space Station. This space station orbits the Earth.

We know that at least one of the planets orbiting the Sun can support life. By studying the Sun, scientists can look for other planets in the **galaxy** that are similar to Earth. One day in the future, these planets might be places that humans could live.

The Sun produces a kind of light called ultraviolet that can not normally be seen. This light is part of what causes sunburns, and it can be harmful to people and animals. Most of the ultraviolet light produced by the Sun is blocked by a part of Earth's atmosphere called the ozone layer. This layer can be damaged by human-made chemicals. Though many of these chemicals are no longer used, damage has already been done to the ozone layer. Sun safety is always important.

Planet Distances

**Eight planets orbit the Sun in our solar system.
Some are close to the Sun, and others are far away.**

PLANETS	AVERAGE DISTANCE FROM THE SUN
MERCURY	36 million miles (58 million km)
VENUS	67 million miles (108 million km)
EARTH	93 million miles (150 million km)
MARS	142 million miles (228 million km)
JUPITER	484 million miles (778 million km)
SATURN	886 million miles (1,427 million km)
URANUS	1,784 million miles (2,871 million km)
NEPTUNE	2,795 million miles (4,498 million km)

Sun Safety

Some people think that having a suntan looks healthy. A suntan is actually damaged skin. Damage to the skin is caused by too much sunlight. Sun damage can lead to skin cancer. It also causes wrinkles. This can make people appear older than they really are. Wearing sunscreen protects the skin from the Sun's rays. Clothing can also protect skin from the sun. Anyone who will be outside for long periods of time, either working or playing, should protect themselves from the Sun's rays.

■ A sunscreen's strength is measured by its sun proof factor (SPF). The higher the SPF, the more protection the sunscreen offers from the Sun's rays.

What is an Astronomer?

An astronomer is a scientist who studies objects in space. This includes stars, galaxies, planets, and giant clouds of gas called nebulae.

Astronomers use many tools to study outer space. Telescopes are one important tool. A telescope can record and show light from objects in space, even in types of light that humans cannot normally see. Some telescopes are based on Earth, usually in areas where the air is dry and clear. Other telescopes orbit the Earth in space. This allows the telescopes to take clearer pictures of the stars. Astronomers also use tools such as radio receivers to measure other types of energy in space.

Neil deGrasse Tyson

Neil Tyson was born in Manhattan, New York, in 1958. Since visiting the Hayden Planetarium in Boston at age 9, he had a strong interest in astronomy. Studying at the universities of Harvard, Texas, and Columbia, he earned a doctorate degree in Astrophysics. Today, he is the director of the Hayden Planetarium and a popular voice promoting science. Tyson has hosted television shows, and he was appointed to assist NASA by President George W. Bush.

EQUIPMENT

Some telescopes are so large that they look like buildings. Some of these are on top of Mauna Kea, the highest mountain in Hawai'i. These telescopes measure light and radio waves.

COMPUTERS

Astronomers collect so much data that no human could ever sort through it all. Instead, astronomers run programs on powerful computers. These programs display the data in ways that are helpful to scientists.

Eight Facts About the Sun

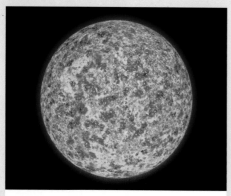

The Sun is more than 4.5 billion years old.

The Sun is a type of star called a **yellow dwarf**.

The Sun's gravity is 28 times stronger than Earth's.

Eight planets, including Earth, orbit the Sun.

Earth could fit inside the Sun about 1 million times.

The Sun makes up 99.8 percent of the solar system's mass.

Light from the Sun takes 8 minutes and 32 seconds to reach Earth.

Light from the Sun is sometimes blocked by the Moon. This is called a solar eclipse.

Sun Brain Teasers

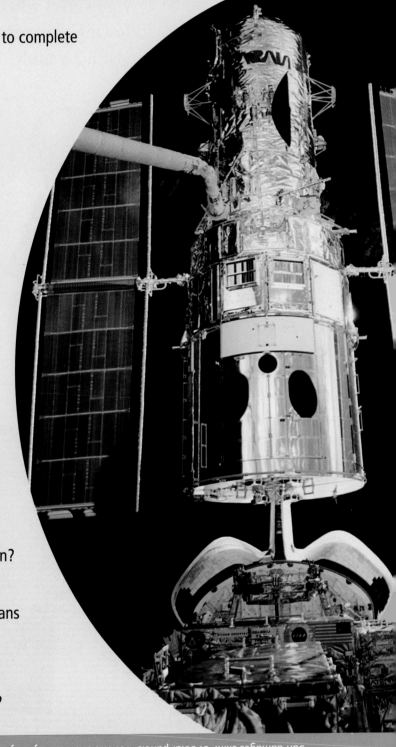

1 How long does it take Earth to complete one orbit around the Sun?

2 What is the name of the star closest to Earth?

3 What did the Egyptians call the Sun god?

4 If you could travel to the Sun, would you be able to walk on its surface?

5 What causes Earth's weather?

6 What kind of star is the Sun?

7 How do monarch butterflies migrate to warm areas?

8 Is sunlight good for your skin?

9 What invention allows humans to use the Sun's energy?

10 Would you like to visit the International Space Station?

ANSWERS: 1. 365.25 days, or one year. **2.** The Sun **3.** Ra **4.** No. The Sun is too hot to walk on. **5.** The Sun warms the air **6.** A yellow dwarf star **7.** Monarch butterflies are guided by the Sun's location in the sky. **8.** Too much Sun damages skin. **9.** Solar panels. **10.** The answer may be yes or no. Give a reason to support your answer.

Cooking with the Sun

The Sun's energy can be very powerful when it is concentrated on a small point. Try the following experiment on a sunny day. This activity should be done with an adult.

Materials Needed

egg

magnifying glass

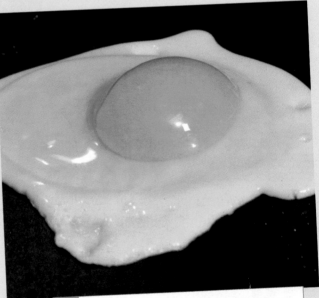
pan or plate

Directions

1 Crack open the egg. Gently drip it into the pan or onto the plate.

2 Place the pan or plate containing the egg in direct, bright sunlight.

3 Move your magnifying glass between the Sun and the plate until the Sun shines through the lens in one small, bright point. Depending on the size of the lens, this may be between 3 and 12 inches.

4 Watch the clear egg begin to turn white. This is the energy of the sun beginning to cook the egg.

Key Words

compass: an instrument that shows directions

core: center of something

fossil fuels: fuels that comes from the bodies of dead plants and animals, such as coal and oil

galaxy: a large group of stars

gravity: force that pulls things toward the center

hydrogen: a light, clear gas that burns easily

migration: travels from one place to another

myth: a story or legend, often about gods or heroes

orbit: the circular path a planet makes around an object in the sky, such as the Sun

satellites: orbiting spacecraft

sunspots: temporary dark spots on the surface of the Sun

telescopes: instruments that make distant objects appear closer

yellow dwarf: a star that gives off a yellow glow

Index

Log on to www.av2books.com

AV² by Weigl brings you media enhanced books that support active learning. Go to www.av2books.com, and enter the special code found on page 2 of this book. You will gain access to enriched and enhanced content that supplements and complements this book. Content includes video, audio, weblinks, quizzes, a slide show, and activities.

Audio
Listen to sections of the book read aloud.

Video
Watch informative video clips.

Embedded Weblinks
Gain additional information for research.

Try This!
Complete activities and hands-on experiments.

WHAT'S ONLINE?

Try This!	Embedded Weblinks	Video	EXTRA FEATURES

Complete a solar power activity. Identify the layers of the Sun. Try a solar system mapping activity. Test your knowledge of the Sun.	Learn more about the Sun. Find out more about the Sun and the solar system. Read more about solar power. Learn more about how the Sun affects the seasons on Earth.	Watch a video about the Sun. Watch a video about the solar system.	**Audio** Listen to sections of the book read aloud.
			
			  Key Words Study vocabulary, and complete a matching word activity.
			
			  Slide Show View images and captions, and prepare a presentation.
			
			  Quizzes Test your knowledge.

AV² was built to bridge the gap between print and digital. We encourage you to tell us what you like and what you want to see in the future.

Sign up to be an AV² Ambassador at www.av2books.com/ambassador.

Pittsburgh Theological Monographs

New Series

Dikran Y. Hadidian
General Editor

19

The Quest for Church Unity
From John Calvin to Isaac d'Huisseau

The Quest for Church Unity

From John Calvin to Isaac d'Huisseau

By
Richard Stauffer

PICKWICK PUBLICATIONS
Allison Park, Pennsylvania

Copyright © 1986 by **Pickwick Publications**
4137 Timberlane Drive, Allison Park, PA 15101

Library of Congress Cataloging-in-Publication Data

Stauffer, Richard, 1921-
    The quest for church unity.

    (Pittsburgh theological monographs; new ser. 19)
    Contents: Calvin, advocate of evangelical Catholicity -- Amyraut, advocate of
reconciliation between Reformed and Lutherans -- D'Huisseau, advocate of reconciliation betweem all Christian confessions.
    1. Christian union -- Reformed Church -- History.
2. Calvin, Jean, 1509-1564. 3. Amyraut, Moise, 1596-1664. 4. Huisseau, Isaac d'. 5.
Reformed Church -- Relations. I. Title. II. Series.
BX9419.5A1S732   1986   270.6   86-1451
ISBN 0-915138-63-8

Contents

Preface

These pages comprise the full written text of the David S. Schaff lectures delivered at Pittsburgh Theological Seminary in April, 1984. This lecture series was the happy occasion of the first visit of Richard and Irene Stauffer to the United States since a student year in New York City some thirty years earlier.

Shortly after their return to France, Professor Stauffer fell ill and died on 9 November 1984 at the age of sixty three. To reformation – and especially to Calvin – studies, the loss of so great a scholar is incalculable.

Richard Stauffer, Swiss born, was a minister of the French Reformed Church in Basel (Switzerland). He was then called to teach Reformation History at the French Protestant Theological Faculty of Paris and became Professor of the History and Theology of the Reformation at l'Ecole Pratique des Hautes Etudes, Sciences Religieuses (Sorbonne). From 1979 to 1983, he was its president. Stauffer received a Docteur es' lettres d'Etat from the University of Paris in 1973 and the Docteur en Theologie from the University of Strasbourg in 1976. He also received honorary degrees from universities in Switzerland and Scotland.

In addition to publishing some 45 articles in scholarly journals and co-authoring 11 books, Professor Stauffer wrote 7 books, some of which have been translated into German, English, Japanese, Spanish, Portuguese, and Korean.

Dr. Stauffer had expected to add an introductory and concluding chapters to this work, but was unable to complete that task. Nevertheless, it is a joy to see these lectures in print. Perhaps more than his other studies, available in English, these lectures demonstrate Richard Stauffer's historical range and precision, his theological acumen, and his ecumenical and confessional sensitivity. They are a valuable legacy from one of the world's outstanding students of the Reformation— a learned, wise, and gentle man.

Charles Partee

PUBLISHER'S NOTE
We should like to express our gratitude to Dr. Donald G. Miller for valuable assistance in the revision of the translation.

Calvin, Advocate of
Evangelical Catholicity

In making of the Genevan Reformer the pioneer of evangelical catholicity, I am not unaware of the reactions to which I may give rise. It may seem paradoxical to affirm that the man who, after the decisive impetus given by Luther, finally established the Reformation upon foundations which have endured until this day was one of the protagonists of Christian unity. [1] And yet, beyond this apparent paradox, there is an undeniable truth. It is that truth which I shall attempt to bring to light. I shall examine, in a first section, the preoccupation with catholicity that was present in Calvin. In a second section, I will show the efforts that he deployed in attempting to regroup the evangelical Christendom of the 16th century. In a third section, lastly, I will bring out the constitutive elements of catholicity retained by Calvin and, in a negative manner, since the 16th century was unfortunately a century of separation for Christendom, the limits of this evangelical catholicity.

I

It has been sometimes affirmed that Calvin owed his preoccupation with the unity of the Church to the teaching that he had received from Bucer, the Strasbourg Reformer, with whom he was associated during the years 1538 to 1541. Such, however is not the case. This concern precedes Calvin's stay in the Alsatian capital. It appears as early as the first edition of the *Institutes of the Christian Religion*, published in 1536. Far more: this concern already inspired the young Calvin; it even prevented him for a time from adhering to the Reformation to which he felt himself attracted. In his *Second Defense ... In Answer to the Calumnies of Westphal*, Calvin imparts to us a strange secret: he there declares that the disputes between Luther and Zwingli turned him away from the evangelical ideal. "Beginning somewhat to leave the darkness of the papacy and having somewhat tasted of sound doctrine, when I read in Luther that Oecolempadius and Zwingli left nothing in the sacraments but nude figures and representations without the truth, I confess that this turned me away from their books, so that I abstained for some time from reading them ..."[2] Calvin pursues his thought by underlining the fact that the divisions among Protestants over eucharistic dogma were scandalous to him.

This concern for unity, this need for catholicity, is manifested by Calvin in the clearest fashion in numerous texts. When he treats, in the *Institutes of the Christian Religion*, for example, the article of the Creed relative to the "holy catholic church," he not only sees in her the invisible church, but indeed the visible church. This visible church is the multitude spread over the world who worship God and Christ, who witness to their faith by baptizing, who affirm its unity in the celebration of the eucharist, who are faithful to the Bible and defend the ministry of preaching. [3] I quote: "Often...the name 'church' designates the whole multitude of man spread over the earth who profess to worship one God and Christ. By baptism we are initiated into faith in him; by partaking in the Lord's Supper we attest our unity in the true doctrine and love; in the Word of the Lord we have agreement, and for the preaching of the Word the ministry instituted by Christ is preserved." [4]

With regard to this visible church, we have the duty to be in communion with her. Calvin does not hesitate to apply the declaration of St. Cyprian: *Extra Ecclesiam nulla salus.* [5] He writes: "Away from her bosom one cannot hope for any forgiveness of sins or any salvation." [6] It is he who, still dependent on St. Cyprian stated in his treatise *De Ecclesiae Catholicae Unitate: Habere non potest Deum patrem, qui Ecclesiam non habet matrem.* [7] Calvin feels that the visible church is the mother of those who have God as their Father. [8] Now this church is one. Otto Weber has very rightly remarked that, in the twenty-nine paragraphs included in the first chapter of Book IV of the *Institutes of the Christian Religion*, nineteen speak of the unity of the church. [9] This is a unity which is due to the fact that Christ is the sole head of the church. A single body, indeed, is concordant with a single head. Commenting on 1 Corinthians 12:12, Calvin asserts that the church, the visible church, is "the mystical and spiritual body of Christ." [10] But the similitude between the head and the body is not the only one used by the Reformer. Echoing Ephesians 5, taking up an expression dear to St. Bernard and to the mystics, he resorts to the similitude of the husband and the wife. To the sole husband that is Christ belongs but one wife: the church. [11]

One might quote other texts which show the obvious fact that Calvin does not extrude catholicity from the evangelical faith. I shall limit myself to only one quotation, from the *Catechism* of 1542/1545. To the master's question: "What is the catholic Church?", the scholar is called upon to respond: it is the company of the faithful that God has ordained and elected to eternal life." And before the master who persues: "Is it necessary to believe this article?" the scholar declares: "Yes it is, if we do not wish to make Christ's death vain, and that which has already been recited, for the fruit which proceeds from it is the Church."[12] If one should retort that these texts refer to Calvin's thought regarding the invisible church which only God knows, it would be necessary to bring out the following portion of the fifteenth section of the same *Cathechism.* To the master who asks: "What means this word catholic, or universal?", the scholar answers: "It is to signify that, as there is but one head of the faithful (Jesus Christ is of course understood here), so all must be united in one body. Such that there are not several Churches, but only one, which is spread over the world." These words are clear; they leave no doubt as to the Reformer's thought: the notion of ecclesiastical pluralism is totally foreign to him.

From that which I have just brought out, the obvious conclusion is that Calvin hates schism. He does not hesitate to say that those who stray from "any Christian company within which there is the ministry of his Word [the word of God, obviously] and of his sacraments" are "traitor[s] and apostate[s] from Christianity."[14] To revolt against the church is to elevate oneself against God himself, to commit the most atrocious of crimes. See on this point the first chapter of Book IV of the *Institutes* entitled: "Of the true Church, with which we must remain united, because she is the mother of all the faithful". See the *Epistle to the King* in which Calvin intends to prove to Francis I that the Reformed are neither rebels nor innovators. See the treatise on *The Necessity of Reforming the Church* where he declares to Charles V: "We have not separated ourselves from the Church and we are not outside of her communion."[15]

But, then, how does Calvin situate the Reformation with respect to the Roman Church? To answer this question, one must descend to the ground of 16th century polemics. In the eyes of the Genevan Reformer, it is indeed a matter of distinguishing between the true and the false Church. The true visible Church may be recognised by two *notes* or two symbols. These two notes, these two symbols, are the pure preaching of the gospel and the administration of the sacraments in conformity with the ordinance of Christ. "Wherever," writes Calvin, "we see the Word of God purely preached and heard, and the sacraments administered according to Christ's institution, it is not to be doubted a church of God exists."[16] As you will have noticed, Calvin simply restates the teaching of Melanchton in article VII of the Augsburg Confession.

Now the two notes that characterize the true church are absent from the "papacy", the French Reformer believes. "Instead of the ministry of the Word, a perverse government compounded of lies rules there, which partly extinguishes the pure light, partly chokes it. The foulest sacrilege has been introduced in place of the Lord's Supper. The worship of God has been deformed by a diverse and unbearable mass of superstitions. Doctrine (apart from which Christianity cannot stand) has been entirely buried and driven out."[17] In painting this very black picture of that which he names the "papacy." Calvin omits speaking of baptism. This is not by chance! As Giovanni Miegge reminded us,[18] baptism is one of these *vestigia ecclesiae,* one of these "Vestiges of the church" which result in that, for Calvin, the Church of Rome, to which he refuses the pure and simple qualification of church (it is precisely for this reason that he calls it the "papacy"), has not however lost all ecclesial character.

Having recalled the doctrine of the "notes" of the Church and having outlined that of its vestiges, I return to my original purpose. These doctrines have as their consequence, in the eyes of the Reformer, that the Roman Church, even if she has conserved baptism, cannot be, is not the catholic church, the universal church founded by Christ. Consequently, (contrary to the Protestants, who, as Jaques Courvoisier has shown,[19] in the 18th century began to find the adjective "catholic" embarrassing), Calvin lays claim to the notion of catholicity. For him, the Reformed have not "snatched away from the Church of Christ,"[20] it is unjustified to accuse them of "schism and heresy,"[21] because they are founded upon the rock of the apostles and the prophets. I quote: "Now let them go and shout that we who have withdrawn from their church are heretics, since the sole cause of our separation is that they could in no way bear the pure profession of truth. I forbear to mention that they have expelled us with anathemas and curses - more than sufficient reason to absolve us, unless they wish to condemn the apostles also as schismatics, whose case was like our own."[22]

Within such a perspective, it is not the Reformed who appear as schismatics, but the "papists" who "disguise themselves under the name of the Church."[23] As one can see, before the schism of the 16th century, Calvin pleads "not guilty". In the treatise on *The Necessity of Reforming the Church*, he goes as far as saying that the "papists" are the sole ones responsible for having torn the seamless robe of the church, that they alone are responsible for having dismembered the body of Christ.

One text seems to me to summarise in a remarkable manner that which I have just outlined. It is taken from the *Reply* that Calvin composed, in 1539/1540, [24] to Cardinal Sadoleto, bishop of Carpentras, a humanist of distinction who was a partisan of disciplinary and moral reformation, and who had written to the Genevans in order to invite them to return to the bosom of the Church. In a somewhat rapid fashion, failing to recognise the authentically religious motives which had brought a certain number of men to raise a sorrowful protest against the ecclesiastical institution of their time, Sadoleto had accused Calvin of being an instigator of schism. To this accusation, the Reformer responded in these terms:[25]

"As to the charge of forsaking the Church, which they were wont to bring against me, there is nothing of which my conscience accuses me unless, indeed, he is to be considered a deserter, who, seeing the soldiers routed and scattered, and abandoning the ranks, raises the leader's standard, and recalls them to their posts. For thus, O Lord, were all thy servants dispersed, so that they could not, by any possibility, hear the command, but had almost forgotten their leader, and their service, and their military oath. In order to bring them together when thus scattered, I raised not a foreign standard, but that noble banner of thine whom we must follow, if we would be classed among thy people."[26]

Having thus proclaimed the legitimacy of his calling -- which rests, according to him, on the fact that he proclaimed nothing other than the gospel -- Calvin treats the difficult question of the responsibility for the schism. Alluding to the Roman hierarchy, he declares: ". . . those who, when they ought to have kept others in their ranks, had led them astray, and when I determined not to desist, opposed me with violence. On this grievous tumults arose, and the contest blazed and issued in disruption. With whom the blame rests it is for Thee, O Lord, to decide. Always, both by word and deed, have I protested how eager I was for unity."[27]

These words must be taken for what they desire to be: a confession before God who knows the thoughts and the hearts. It is out of the question for us to use these words for settling the problem of the share of responsibilities in the schism of the 16th century. It belongs to God to judge, and without doubt he considers all of us guilty! On the other hand, the remarks of Calvin in the *Reply to Sadoleto* can recall to us the dramatic conflict of conscience which was posed before numerous believers in the 16th century, and the acute sense of catholicity, the need of unity, which never ceased to characterize the Reformers.

II

"Always, by both word and deed, have I protested how eager I was for unity." These words of Calvin bring us to the second section. We will here see how the Reformer tried to achieve, for want of a union which would have gathered all Christians in one catholic reformed church, an evangelical catholicity, which, with the Reformed, would have included the Zwinglians, the Lutherans, the Anglicans, and all those who, in the respect of the established forms, intended to profess that which was then called the "pure Gospel of Jesus Christ".

Let us speak first of all of the efforts made by Calvin, with regard to the disciples of Zwingli, the Reformer of Zürich and a good share of German-speaking Switzerland. As everyone knows, Zwingli and Luther opposed one another at the Marburg Colloquy on the question of the presence of Christ in the eucharist. In agreement on all other points, they were unable to agree on this particular question. I recall to your attention the fifteenth and last article of Marburg: "Even though we were presently unable to agree on the question of knowing whether the true body and the true blood of the Lord are corporally (*leiblich*) present in the bread and the wine of the Supper, each side will however testify Christian charity to the other, as much as its conscience will permit . . . ."[28] Behind this formation which was an attempt to save face, one can guess the point of contention which set the Wittenberg Reformer against his Zürich colleague. While Luther insisted on the words "This is my body" and underlined the real presence of Christ in, with and under the elements of the bread and the wine, Zwingli put the accent on the terms "Do this in remembrance of me" and brought out the memorial character of the supper.

Faced with these divergences, Calvin attempted to play the role of mediator. He took this mission upon himself all the more easily since

his conception of the eucharist appeared to reconcile the true intentions of Luther and of Zwingli. With Luther, the French Reformer
intended to give justice to the religious profundity of the supper: he
could not satisfy himself with the Zwinglian memorial. With Zwingli,
he could not admit the "materialist" conception of corporal presence
defended by many a Lutheran. He attempted therefore to defend
Luther and the Lutherans before the Zwinglians, and to make himself
the advocate of the latter against Lutheran extremists.

His irenic stance in this affair was manifested in his *Short Treatise on
the Supper of our Lord,* of 1541. Written in French, this short treatise
unfortunately was not translated into Latin until 1545 so that Luther
only became acquainted with it a short time before his death! The Wittenberg Reformer made no mistake. If one is to believe Christopher
Pezel, one of his confidants, Luther recognized that he could have
entrusted Calvin with the defense of his conceptions; he admitted
that, if Oecolampadius and Zwingli had expressed themselves in the
terms of the French Reformer, there would never have been a eucharistic quarrel among the Protestants. According to Pezel, Luther stated
concerning Calvin, after having scanned his treatise on the Supper:
"This is certainly a learned and pious man; I could have, at the beginning entrusted to him the whole affair in this debate. For myself, I
recognise that, if the opposing party had done the same, we could
have soon come to an agreement. For if Oecolampadius and Zwingli
had thus expressed themselves at the beginning, we would have
never arrived at such a long dispute."[29]

But Calvin did not limit himself to composing the *Short Treatise on
the Supper of our Lord.* Seeing the relations between Lutherans and
Zwinglians become more and more embittered, he spared neither
time nor effort in attempting to repair the breach that had thus opened
in Protestantism's flank. Unable to reunite in one stroke those who
were separated on this eucharistic question, he conceived first of a
reconciliation with the partisans of Zwingli. The idea was attractive.
Continental Protestantism was divided at that time into three spiritual
families, gravitating around Wittenberg, Zürich and Geneva. Reconciling Geneva and Zürich would reduce the movements born of the
Reformation from three to two. Even more, it was a first step toward
the constitution of an evangelical catholicity.

Calvin therefore entered into relations with Bullinger, Zwingli's
successor. After a long exchange of correspondence, and after serious

theological reflection (lasting several years), the two men concluded, in the name of their Churches, the famous Zurich Agreement of 1549.[30] Important in its content (it surpassed indeed Zwinglian symbolism in affirming that God accomplishes truly in us, by his Holy Spirit, that which the sacraments typify before our eyes and senses), it was decisive in its repercussions on the history of Protestantism. Henceforth, as Emile Doumergue remarked, the sons of the Reformation were, on the Continent, grouped into two families.[31]

But this, for Calvin, should have been but a first step. To his great sorrow, however, the *Zürich Agreement*, which, owing to the support of the Genevans, should have cleared the disciples of Zwingli in the eyes of the Lutherans, was not understood in Germany. It contained indeed one article, article XXIV, which was prone to shock the Lutherans. After having condemned the "foolish imagination of the Papists" as to Transubstantiation, this article added: "We deem it no less absurd to place Christ under the bread or couple him with the bread, than to transubstantiate the bread into his body."[32]

Insensitive to the fact that the *Zürich Agreement* was to prepare a wider concord, to prepare a more genuine fraternity among Protestants, the disciples of Luther showed themselves perhaps more uncompromising than their teacher. They spared no criticism in attacking Calvin. The latter, however, remained convinced to the end of his career that if Luther had lived longer, he would have assented to the *Zürich Agreement*. He thus wrote, in 1554, to Marbach, pastor in Strasbourg: "If this excellent servant of God and faithful doctor of the Church, Martin Luther, were yet alive, he would not be as severe and implacable as to refuse his assent to this confession, namely that that which the sacraments represent is truly given, and that, in consequence, we participate in the Supper in the body and the blood of Christ. How often Luther said that he fought for nothing other than this, namely that the lord does not mock us with empty signs."[33] And, several years later, in 1560, the Genevan Reformer wrote to Rector Matthias Schenck of Augsburg: "Wittenberg has produced, I confess, several pious and courageous personalities. But the majority believe themselves to be faithful imitators of Luther by inflating themselves with pretentious arrogance instead of the openness of mind which this man possessed. The same thing came about in Jerusalem, when, at the time of the apostles, true piety was flourishing and esteemed. For there were no worse enemies of the Gentile-Christian communities than those who come from Jerusalem and pretended to be the true disciples of James and of the others.'[34]

After the efforts deployed by Calvin on the Zwinglian side, which, if one considers but these, were crowned with success, the steps undertaken by the Reformed in the direction of the Lutherans merit as well a brief examination. We note first that it is not for merely tactical reasons that Calvin sought after union with German Protestantism. During his stay in Strasbourg, the French Reformer had had the occasion to participate, side by side with Lutheran theologians, in the Colloquies of Haguenau, Worms, and Ratisbon, which, as Pierre Fraenkel has shown,[35] appear to us today as the great occasions of the 16th century where Protestants and Papists could have come to agreement. In the course of these encounters, Calvin had developed solid friendships among the Lutherans, with Melanchthon in particular. Even more than this, in order to participate in these encounters, and to represent Strasbourg, he had to sign that charter of Lutheranism, the Augsburg Confession, not, as it has often been claimed, in its 1540 version, the *Confessio Augustana Variata*, but in its primitive version, as Willem Nijenhuis has shown,[36] the *Invariata* of 1530.

Thus, strong ties linked Calvin to the moderate Lutherans. It is through them, through Melanchthon especially, that he attempted to win German Protestantism over to the cause of evangelical catholicity. But Melanchthon was not one to influence his coreligionists in a lasting fashion. The most substantial step that he took in the path of reconciliation was perhaps the modification that he brought in 1540 to article X of the Augsburg Confession, relative to the Lord's Supper, in a direction which was to facilitate the rallying of the Protestants of Upper Germany and of the "middle-of-the-roaders".[37]

All of this was quite cautious. And, moreover, all of this, was called into question after the promulgation of the *Zürich Agreement*. From 1549 to 1556, a pastor from Hamburg, named Westphal, enlisted in the service of his theological ill-temper a tireless pen: he took Calvin to task, culpable in his eyes of having compromised with the disciples of Zwingli. And Calvin, who, in polemics, knew how to use biting sarcasm, responded in the same tone to the ranter who was maltreating him. This was far from Evangelical catholicity; and the spectacle of these fighting Protestants, from the perspective of four centuries, is not very edifying to contemplate.

It would be an error, however, to think that Calvin was content with these quarrels. Although, carried away by his controversialist temperament, he engaged himself in a one-way dialogue with Westphal, at the same time he yearned for unity. Even more, he sought by every possible means to unite the sons of the Reformation in a genuine communion. The best proof of what I here advance is that one year after the controversy with Westphal, in 1557, Calvin dispatched two ambassadors to Germany. He chose them with the greatest care. These were William Farel, his elder and his friend, and Theodore Beza, later his successor in Geneva. After having visited the Swiss cantons, these two men were to come to Strasbourg and Heidelberg. Their mission had but one goal: to prove to the Lutherans that the Reformed see in the supper something other than a symbol; to show them that they there receive the body and the blood of Christ, and having proved this to them, to ask them to consider the Reformed as brothers.

Thus, at a period when travel was difficult, Calvin commissioned his representatives to the German Protestants. Having scarcely returned from their expedition, Beza and Farel set out again for Worms, in the same year, 1557. And when Farel, decidedly too old to go on the road, had to confine himself to his Neuchâtel parish, Beza continued these reconciliatory missions (there will be no less than four of them up until 1559). Each time, the question is that of unity, which, to take up the terms of an address from the Protestant princes of Germany to the king of France, probably composed by Calvin, must exist among all those who keep "the doctrine of the catholic Church of our Lord Jesus Christ contained in the books of the prophets and the apostles, in the creeds and the ancient doctors."[38]

In the light of these repeated and finally vain efforts, one might be tempted to think that Calvin was persuing illusions, and that as these illusions progressively faded away, he remained obstinate in his dream. One might also believe that Calvin's need for unity, his desire for an evangelical catholicity, was a state of mind without any practical bearing. This is not at all the case. We have a letter of 1554, addressed to the English in Wesel, Germany, which offers all desirable clarity on this point. To these Englishmen who had to leave their fatherland under the reign of Bloody Mary because of their evangelical convictions, and who, having taken refuge in Germany, were tempted not to attend the Lutheran worship service because it had retained the use of candles and the communion wafer, Calvin suggests that one must not create division for a few ceremonies which do not imperil the essence of the faith.

Here are a few extracts from this surprising epistle: "Inasmuch as you are but a single member, not only can you lawfully, but also must you endure and suffer such infirmities that are not in your power to correct. We do not esteem that to have lighted candles in the Supper and figurative bread (-wafer) are indifferent things neither for consenting to them nor for approving them, but we have to accomodate ourselves to the use that will already have been accepted regarding them, when we have no authority to remedy it ... although we should come to some place where there would be a different form, there is not one of us, who, through spite of a candle or of a chasuble, would separate himself from the body of the Church, and by this means deprive himself of the supper. We must keep ourselves from scandalizing those who are yet tied to such an infirmity, lest you should reject them for too trivial a cause ... We must accomodate ourselves one to another in all those ceremonies which do not prejudice the confession of our faith, in order that the unity of the Church might not be dissipated through our too great rigor or peevishness."[39] Beside showing the practical range of the overtures made by Calvin to the Lutherans, this text is interesting. It shows that the French Reformer did not see sufficient reasons for secession in liturgical forms which he felt debatable but did not veil evangelical truth.

I have spoken of the efforts directed by Calvin toward the disciples of Zwingli and Luther. We must say a word as well about his relations with the Church of England. For it is here perhaps that his desire for catholicity is most manifest, a catholicity which, while desiring to submit itself entirely to the gospel, means to be respectful of quite diverse ecclesiastical structures. In the important correspondance that he exchanged from 1548 with Edward Seymour, Duke of Somerset and Protector of England,[40] Calvin outlines for the church of that country a program of reformation, "of full and entire reformation", as he says, which includes three points: "The first will be a method to indoctrinate the people well. The second will be the extirpation of the abuses which heretofore prevailed. The third to correct carefully vice, and to see that scandals and disruptions be no wise in fashion, to such extent that the name of God be blasphemed."[41]

To "indoctrinate the people" is to preach the gospel. But in order that there be faithful and informed preachers, Calvin felt it was necessary for the Church of England to give itself "a resolute summary of doctrine that all must preach," that is to say, a confession of faith which expresses in up to date language the eternal truths of the gospel. It is necessary too that this church work out "a common formulary of instruction for small children and the rude among the people," that is, a catechism which puts within the reach of the simplest ones the mysteries of the faith. In order to "indoctrinate the people," it is necessary, finally, for the French Reformer, that the Church possess a lively liturgy, capable of uniting all the believers into one body.

If this first point be established, the two others will be quite normally derived from it, in the view of Calvin. The abolition of that which he names "the abuses and corruptions" consists of renouncing relics, prayer for the departed, and the sacrament of extreme unction: in brief, manifesting "moderation" in the ceremonies. As for the repression of scandals and the punishment of vice, these would be realised in the exercise of a freely asserted to discipline and in a sanctification of marriage which must be "the living image of the sacred union which we have with the Son of God."

You have noticed that there is not one word in this program against the hierarchical structure of the Church of England. Calvin does not question the episcopal ministry. He does not contest the office of the bishops, provided that they discharge their pastoral functions, provided that they preach the gospel. The evangelical catholicity to which the Reformer aspires does not imply the adoption of the ecclesiastical regime that circumstances imposed upon Geneva in the 16th century. It has even been affirmed by the historian Jacques Pannier [42] (a Protestant whose adherence to the Reformation was without reservation) that a certain episcopate is the "organic element of the church in integral Calvinism". Concerning Calvin's relations with the Church of England, one other fact must be mentioned. In 1552, archbishop Cranmer made plans to assemble in England or elsewhere "a synod of the most learned and best men" with the aim of serving the "Christian Republic". The intention of the primate of the Church of England was to establish that doctrinal harmony which could lay the foundation of the unity of the churches born of the Reformation. Consulted by Cranmer himself on the utility and the expediency of such a plan, Calvin concurred without reservation. Here is what he wrote to the primate of England: "May it please God that the learned and serious men of the principal Churches be assembled and having defined with care the principal points of the faith, to deliver to posterity a solid doctrine of Scripture composed from common opinion. Among the greatest evils of our time, one must count the fact that the churches are thus separated one from another, in such fashion that there is hardly even a human relationship among us, in any case that holy communion of Christ's members, of which many boast in words but few sincerely search after in reality does not shine forth. In such manner that, because the members are torn apart, the body of the Church bleeds, lies wounded. As much as is in me, if anyone judges that I be of some utility, I will not be afraid of crossing ten seas for the sake of this, if it be necessary."[43]

If, in his concern for unity, Calvin approached the Zwinglians with success, if he vainly multiplied his advances toward the Lutherans, if he proposed to the Anglicans a program of reformation that took into consideration the conditions particular to England, he also outlined an entire plan of reformation for Poland. It is thus that, in his letter to king Sigismund-Augustus, he shows himself favorable to maintaining the hierarchy (hierarchy in service, of course) if this hierarchy accepts the gospel. Basing his position on the existence of patriarchates in the ancient church, [44] he admits the legitimacy of the archepiscopate, and archepiscopate which, not as a synonym of dominance but of chairmanship, is the unifying link between the diverse bishops.[45]

One last word to terminate the second part of this explanation! It is known to what extent Calvin reacted vigorously to the first sessions of the Council of Trent. In 1547, two years after the convocation of this Council, he published its Proceedings with, as the title of his work stated, "the remedy for the poison." [46] He blamed the Council essentially for being incapable, as it was convened by the Pope, of contributing to the "amending of the Church," and for being incapable of establishing the truth by basing itself on the sole testimony of Holy Scripture.

Now, curiously, something that shows that Calvin had not resigned himself to the division of the Christians in spite of the distrust that those first periods of the Council of Trent (1545-1547 and 1551-1552) provoked within him, he welcomed positively the article of the treaty of Cateau-Cambre'sis (1559) which "stipulated the convening of a general council for the reformation of abuses and the re-establishment of religious unity in Europe."[47] Far from considering that this plan, elaborated by the counselors of Philip II and Henry II, should be rejected definitively, he sent to the Reformed Churches of France, during the year 1560, a *Judgement on the Holding of a Council*. It is not without benefit at this juncture to quote its essential passages:

"To put an end to the divisions which exist within Christendom, it is needful to have a free and universal council (this is the request that Luther had already formulated!). This freedom consists of three points: that is, the place, the persons and the manner of proceeding. As for the place, if there be no sure access for all those who must be heard for debating the subjects which are controverted, it is obvious that the door is closed . . . Touching the persons, . . . it would be an iniquitous thing that there be but the bishops who have a decisive voice seeing that they are partial and therefore cannot be considered competent . . . The remedy would be that there be people elected on the side of those who desire and request the reformation of the Church both in doctrine and in morals . . . As to the procedure, it would be completely frustrative, if one followed that to which we have been accustomed formerly, that is, that those who desire reformation would propose by word of mouth or in writing, and that in their absence Messrs. the prelates give orders as they please. It is therefore required that all be there present, in order that that which would be poorly informed be straightened, and that it be lawful to reply against all erroneous opinions through good and very conclusive reasonings."[48]

You have noticed that though the tone of this *Opinion* is firm, it does not here signify a desire for a definitive break with the papacy. "I have always shown in words and in deeds what desire I had for union and concord," declares Calvin in his *Reply to Sadoleto*. The few historical reminders that I have just given, it seems to me, prove the authenticity of these words. On the level of the Reformation at least, Calvin was never able to accomodate himself to the divisions among Christians. Calvinism (to employ a term that would have horrified the Genevan

(Reformer) did not cease, due in a good part of the 16th century, to wish for, even more to encourage every possible measure, the advent of evangelical catholicity.

III

We must now examine the conditions of catholicity for Calvin. Let us point out first of all that he would have refused most energetically to be considered as the father of a specific "denomination," as the ancestor of one "confession" among others. In his *Réponse a un cauteleux moyenneur . . . ("Answer to a cunning middleman"*, where he intended to combat François Baudoin), the Genevan Reformer considers as an insult the name "Calvinists" that certain of his adversaries gave to his partisans. The term "Calvinist" seems to him as "odious" as that of "anti-Catholic."[49] Why this reaction on Calvin's part? Because his objective was to contribute, on his part, with the gifts that he believed to have received from heaven, to the reformation of the entire church. That he did not succeed in his undertaking, that his plan was not able to be fulfilled, should not let us forget that his attitude is directly opposite to particularism and denominational narrowness. Such an affirmation will certainly not fail to surprise many. Calvin has a poor reputation, including the Protestants who have little love for him. He is reputed to be narrow minded, and even autocratic. In reality, if the author of the *Institutes of the Christian Religion* showed himself to be intransigent when it seemed to him that the faith was in peril, he possessed an extraordinary flexibility in those areas where he felt that the central core of the gospel was not put in doubt. Thus, in his relations with the Zwinglians, the Lutherans, and the Anglicans, he was able to make numerous and perhaps in the eye of some, dangerous concessions.

In order to understand this attitude which, in its manifestations of rigor and of openness, of intransigence and of flexibility, appears contradictory, indeed incoherent, we must remember that Calvin bases his position on a distinction somewhat forgotten today - the distinction between fundamental doctrines and secondary doctrines. This distinction, it seems, was known to Calvin already very shortly after his first ministry at Geneva, which was terminated by his expulsion in 1538. After his forced departure, his partisans and those of Farel, the

Guillermins, were opposed to new pastors named by the magistrate. But Calvin, far from encouraging his partisans toward secession, exhorted them to remain in the communion of the Reformed Church. He held, indeed, that, if this church reinstated certain *reliquae ignorantiae,* she taught just the same *praecipua christianae religionis capita, quae ad salutem sunt necessaria,* [50] that is, the essential points, or the fundamental principles of the Christian religion which are necessary to salvation. These essential points constitute "the doctrine which founds the Church of Christ" (*doctrina qua Ecclesia Christi fundatur*).

Although present in the argument of Calvin when he addresses himself to the Guillermins, the distinction between fundamental articles and secondary articles appears in the most explicit manner in the 1539 edition of the *Institutes of the Christian Religion* (to which the first French edition of this work corresponds, which dates from 1541). This distinction is there found in two passages which will be retained until the last editions of the *Institutes,* the Latin of 1559 and the French of 1560. Thus we read in Book IV, in the first chapter (where the subject is often that of union which "we must keep with the true Church, mother of all the faithful"), ¶ 12: "Not all the articles of true doctrine are of the same sort. Some are so necessary to know that they should be certain and unquestioned by all men as to the proper principles of religion. Such are: God is one; Christ is God and the Son of God; our salvation rests in God's mercy; and the like. Among the churches there are other articles of doctrine disputed which still do not break the unity of faith. Suppose that one church believes - short of unbridled contention and opinionated stubborness - that souls upon leaving bodies fly to heaven; while another, not daring to define the place, is convinced nevertheless that they live in the Lord. What churches would disagree on this point?"

The second text of the *Institutes* relative to the distinction between fundamental articles and secondary articles is found in Book IV, chapter II, ¶ 1. After having shown in this passage that "the ministry of the word of God and of the sacraments" must be valued and that "a few minor faults... in doctrine" do not invalidate this, Calvin adds: "...the errors which ought to be pardoned are those which do not harm the chief doctrine of religion, which do not destroy the articles of religion on which all believers ought to agree."

Calvin adds that, for the "subjects which are not greatly necessary," there must not be *dissidii materia* among Christians; literally: cause of division, "trouble" and "sedition" says the French edition.

To these two passages of the *Institutes of the Christian Religion,* one might add other quotations taken from the *Commentaries* of the Reformer. I shall limit myself to bringing out two texts. The first is taken from the commentary on I Cor. 1:2. Calvin there brings out that the Corinthians, in spite of certain errors and "a little vice," constituted a church because "they retained fundamental doctrine, that one God was worshipped among them and called upon the name of Christ, and that they put in Christ confidence unto salvation, that they also had the ministry which was in no wise corrupted."[51] The second text to be quoted is taken from the commentary on I Cor. 3:11. The Reformer there declares: "The fundamental doctrine, which it is in no way permissible to corrupt, is that we learn Christ. For Christ is the unique foundation of the Church."[52]

The texts relative to the distinction between fundamental articles and secondary articles, be they taken from the *Institutes of the Christian Religion* or from the *Commentaries,* pose certain problems. I here bring out a few of them. There is first of all the difficulty that one senses, in following Calvin, in compiling an exhaustive list of the fundamental articles. I recall to your attention the text of the *Institutes* (IV/I/12) which I highlighted earlier. After having enumerated, in the fundamental articles, the oneness of God, the divinity of Christ and redemption solely in him, this text adds without any other explanation: "and other similar things" (*et similia*). Clearly the Reformer does not sense the need for compiling a complete catalogue of the fundamental articles, as will be attempted later by the irenic Reformer, for example, François Du Jon, in his *Eirenicum* of 1593, and David Pareus, in his *Irenicum* of 1614/1615 [53] or the representatives of Lutheran orthodoxy Matthias Hafenreffer, in his *Loci Theologici,* or Leonhard Hutter, in several of his writings.[54]

Is it a weakness in Calvin, this incapacity, or rather, this desire not to enumerate all the fundamental articles? In the eyes of Otto Weber, no. For the German theologian, Calvin abstained from drawing up a catalogue of the fundamental points in order to hinder the formulation of the faith from congealing itself into a "doctrine," in order to incite the faithful to return always to the living stream of the Scriptures [55]. Assuming that one accepts the answer of Otto Weber, another question must be posed: What is the "central core," if I may so state it, of the fundamental articles? We can respond without hesitating, I believe, that this "central core" is the very content of the message of the Reformation: the doctrine of salvation in Jesus Christ. The "principal doctrine of our religion," to take up the terms of the *Institutes,* the "fundamental doctrine" par excellence, is: Jesus Christ, the only Savior.

From what I have just stated, it follows that, for Calvin, ecclesial unity is not necessarily doctrinal uniformity to the smallest detail. There is a fringe, narrow of course, where, without breaking the communion bond, believers may differ in their opinions. This is not here a question of a naive frame of mind. Thus, as is shown by the *Institutes of the Christian Religion,* the Reformer who had a lively interest in the destiny of the departed (the best proof of this is that his first theological work, the *Psychopannychia* of 1534, dealt with this problem and showed, against the Anabaptists, that after death souls do not sleep in awaiting the last judgement), held that the different manners of conceiving life after death, whether an immediate transfer to heaven or an existence in God, should not shatter the unity of the Church.

To take another example, which touches 20th century Protestants more directly perhaps than that of the destiny of the souls of which the *Institutes* speak, I would say that the presbytero-synodal system which has prevailed in the Reformed Churches does not constitute for Calvin what was at stake in the Reformation. The Genevan Reformer never mentions the presbytero-synodal system as a fundamental article. If the episcopate had, in France or elsewhere, embraced the evangelical ideal in the 16th century, the Reformation would have been inscribed in the framework of the traditional hierarchy.

Having drawn the secret of his flexibility, the explanation of his surprising openness in many a circumstance, from the distinction that Calvin makes between fundamental and secondary articles, I would like to bring out now that which, in his search for unity and in his strong desire for catholicity, appears to him as being decisive.

The "principal doctrine of our religion," the fundamental articles, all of this has its source in the Bible, and in the Bible alone. Thus, the unity of the Church has as its first condition submission to Scripture. The Reformation claims to be catholic because it claims to plunge its roots in the biblical revelation, because it claims to be founded upon the testimony of the apostles and the prophets. The principle of *sola Scriptura,* on which Calvin insisted even more than Luther, appears to him as the sole legitimate foundation of the church, as the platform from which she must not deviate unless she were to decline or to fall.

The second condition of catholicity resides for Calvin (this follows from that which I have noted above) in reverence for the lordship of

Jesus Christ. It was affirmed throughout the 19th century that the Reformer of Geneva was, in an exclusive sense, the theologian of the *soli Deo gloria*. The point was thus made that he had exalted the omnipotence, magnified the transcendence, of God. And, in this perspective, the importance of the dogma of double-predestination was exaggerated, misunderstanding the fact that in the 16th century this dogma was for believers a source of assurance and of joy: it did not evoke damnation for them, but rather the mysterious and gracious election that God acccorded to them in his Son.

Thus I return to that which I said earlier, that it is not in rediscovering the doctrine of God, but that of Christ, that Calvin became a Reformer. It is the merit of the dialectical thought originating in Karl Barth to have seen that Calvin was not only the theologian of the first article, but that he had given a considerable place to Christology, and that beyond appearances he was the cantor of the grace and mercy of God. In a work now become classic,[56] Wilhelm Niesel has shown the decisive role that Jesus Christ, the incarnate Word plays in Calvinist dogmatics. Founded, then upon the Son of God, calling upon him alone to the exclusion of any human intermediary, the Reformation affirms and proclaims itself catholic.

This claim of catholicity was contested by the Romanist theologians of the 16th century. Today, it is infinitely better understood by those of their successors who are interested in the Reformation. To speak of but one of Calvin's interpreters, I point out, for example, that Alexandre Ganoczy has been extremely sensitive to the Genevan Reformer's sense of catholicity. Ganoczy writes: "Calvin insistently advocates a return to Christ through the Gospel, a return which presupposes the continuity of the Church and is opposed to all 'novelty'."[57] And further on: "Calvin... never intended to break with that which is most essential in the catholic doctrine of the Church. Likewise, he never thought that it was necessary, by means of a 'salutary amputation', to oppose a new Church to the old."[58]

The authority of Scripture and the lordship of Christ, heart of the Reformation and the reason for its affirmation of catholicity! But what are the limits that are negatively implied by such a conception of catholicity? To this question, Calvin gives a sharp response. For him, all those are excluded from the catholic church, who, straying from the Scripture by making allowance for tradition, even the most minimal one, succeed automatically, in his eyes, in distancing themselves from the Lord Christ. In this answer, Calvin focuses upon two attitudes that are generally considered as completely antagonistic. These two attitudes are those of two adversaries against whom the Reformation fought with the fiercest energy: on the right wing, if you permit, the Roman Church; on the left wing, Anabaptism.

Calvin thinks that, through her recourse to tradition, to the traditions, the Roman Church ends in erecting a hierarchy, and finally, the papacy, as supreme authority to the detriment of the lordship of Christ. Of course, Calvin does not ignore the promises of assistance that Christ made to his church. He holds, however, that these never constitute for the church a guaranty of infallibility. According to him, the truth is always to be received from the Holy Spirit who always speaks through Scripture. *Spiritus in Verbo operans.* Never can the church pretend to hold and possess this Spirit outside of scriptural revelation. The cutting edge of the critique that Calvin addresses to the Roman Church is that, whenever the decisions of her magisterium stray from the biblical given, she is purely and simply the victim of illuminism.

Accusing the Roman Church of illuminism, and illuminism concentrated, if I might say, in the person of the Pope, Calvin pronounces the same accusation against Anabaptism. Anabaptism? Just as much as the papacy, it was the "pet aversion" of the Reformers. We know of Luther's hostility toward those that he names the Schwärmer. It is less well-known that Zwingli felt (in a letter addressed to Vadian 28 May, 1525) that the struggle to be waged on the "second front," as he calls it, that is, against the Anabaptists, is infinitely more difficult than the one which-"child's play"- must be conducted against the Roman Church. Calvin shares the animosity of Luther and of Zwingli toward Anabaptism, an animosity which, today, does not appear to us as entirely justified. Indeed, when they speak of Anabaptism, the reformers practice the method of amalgamation. They gather into one and the same category people or groups quite different- Zürich Baptists, for example, and the partisans of Thomas Müntzer or the insurgents of Münster. Also, where Calvin and the other Reformers speak of Anabaptism, it would be more accurate to use the term "spiritualists" or better, "illuminati."

Having given these few details, we must observe that, under the name of "Anabaptism," Calvin aims at a movement, or movements, which constituted a serious threat for the Reformation - a serious threat, because they tended to avoid Scripture in favor of a direct inspiration of believer, because they exalted the religious individual at the expense, often, of the lordship of Christ. These movements, without any doubt, merit the accusation of illuminism made against them.

The reduction of the Roman Church and of Anabaptism to the same denominator, the accusation that the one and the other proceed from illuminism, is already found in Luther's writings, in a striking passage of the *Smalcald Articles,* published in German during the summer of 1538.[59] In an independent fashion, it would seem - since he did not know German - Calvin effectuates the same reduction, by proceeding to make the same identification in his *Reply to Cardinal Sadoleto's Letter* of 1539/1540. He there declares: ". . . whenever the prophets foretell the renewal of the Church, or its extension over the whole globe, they always assign the first place to the Word . . . does Chrysotom admonish us to reject all who, under the pretence of the Spirit, lead us away from the simple doctrine of the gospel - the Spirit having been promised not to reveal a new doctrine, but to impress the truth of the gospel on our minds. And we, in fact, experience in the present day how necessary the admonition was. We are assailed by two sects, which seem to differ most widely from each other. For what similitude is there in appearance between the Pope and the Anabaptists? And yet, that you may see that Satan never transforms himself so cunningly as not in some measure to betray himself, the principle weapon with which they both assail us is the same. For when they boast extravagently of the Spirit, the tendency certainly is to sink and bury the Word of God, that they may make room for their own falsehoods. And you, Sadoleto, by stumbling on the very threshold, have paid the penalty of that affront which you offered to the Holy Spirit when you separated Him from the Word."[60]

Illuminism, therefore, which disjoins the spirit from Scripture, and which, thanks to this disjunction, beclouds the unique lordship of Christ to the advantage of man - this illuminism is, for Calvin, outside of evangelical catholicity. This attitude of the Genevan Reformer is also found in Luther. It is constant in the 16th century. The centers of the Reformation set back to back the Roman Church and the so-called Anabaptists.

Thus, to the flexibility of Calvin, who in order to attain unity, is ready to yield on points that appear to him as secondary is added, inseparable from it, an absolute intransigence on the principles that I have just brought out. Evangelical catholicity as Calvin conceived of it implies limits and even anathemas. The 16th century is a period of tearing apart and of rupture where the organic unity of the body of Christ is definitively compromised. The Genevan Reformer was a man of his time. He did not think otherwise than his contemporaries. His total obedience to that which he held to be truth motivated him to consider as more or less inevitable the division which, today, appears to us as scandalous and intolerable.

Notes

1. On the problem taken up in this chapter cf. Jean Cadier, "Calvin, homme de l'union des Eglises," in *La Revue réformée*, 52, 1962/64, pp 11-20; Günter Gloede, "Calvinus oecumenicus," in *Johannes Calvin*, Berlin, 1963, pp 9-26: Gottfried W. Locher, *Calvin Anwalt der Ökumene*, Zollikon, 1960: John T. McNeill, "Calvin as an Ecumenical Churchman," in *Church History*, 1963/64 and *Unitive Protestantism: The Ecumenical Spirit and its Persistent Expression*, Richmond, 2nd ed. 1964; Willem Nijenhuis, *Calvinus Oecumenicus: Calvin en de eenheid der kerk in het licht van zijn briefwisseling*, La Haye, 1958; G. Reichel, *Calvin als Unionsmann*, Tubingen, 1909; and Otto Weber, *"Die Einheit der Kirche bei Calvin,"* in *Calvin-Studien* 1959, ed. by Jurgen Moltmann, Neukirchen, 1960, pp 130-143.

2. *Recueil des opuscules, c'est-à-dire petits traités de M. Jean Calvin*, Geneva, 1566, p 1503.

3. On the important and often ignored role that the pastoral ministry plays in the Calvinist definition of the church, cf. L. Schümmer, *Le Ministere pastoral dans l'Institution chre'tienne de Calvin à la lumiére du troisième sacrement*, Wiesbaden, 1965

4. *Institution of the Christian Religion*, (henceforth abreviated: ICR), tr. by Ford Lewis Battles, (The Library of Christian Classics, 20-21), Philadelphia: The Westminster Press, 1960. IV/I/ p, 1021

5. *Ep.* 73, XXI; *Ep.* 4, IV, 3

6. *ICR* IV/I/4 p. 1016

7. *Op. Cit.*, ed. of Pierre de Labriolle, Paris, 1942, ¶ 6, p. 12

8. Cf, *ICR* IV/I/1 p. 1012

9. Cf. *art. cit.*, p. 131

10. *Commentaires sur le Nouveau Testament*, Vol. 3, Paris, 1855, p. 451b

11. Cf. *ICR* IV/I/10 and IV/VIII/13.

12. *Bekenntnisschriften und Kirchenordnungen der nach Gottes Wort reformierten Kirche*, ed. by Wilhelm Niesel, Zollikon-Zurich, 2nd ed. n.d. pp 12-13

13. *Ibid.*, p. 13

14. *ICR* IV/I/10 p. 1024

15. *Calvini Opera* (henceforth abbreviated: CO), Vol. VI, col. 519

16. *ICR* IV/I/9 p. 1023

17. *ICR* IV/II/2 p. 1042

18. Cf. "Vestigia Ecclesiae, signes de l'Église dans les Églises," in: *Verbum Caro*, 43, Neuchâtel, 1957, pp. 200-212

19. Cf. *De la Réforme au protestantisme. Essai d'ecclesiologie réformée*, Paris, 1977, p. 190
20. *ICR* IV/II/2 p. 1042
21. *ICR* IV/II/5 p. 1046
22. *ICR* IV/II/6 p. 1047
23. *ICR* III/XXII/4 p. 936
24. 1539: Latin Edition; 1540: French Edition
25. Even though August Lang (cf. "Die Bekehrung Johannes Calvin," in: *Studien zur Geschichte der Theologie und der Kirche*, vol. 2/1, Leipzig, 1897, p. 31 ff) and Karl Müller (cf. "Calvins Bekehrung," in: Nachrichten der Gesellschaft der Wissenschaften Göttingen; Philologisch-historische Klasse, Göttingen, 1905, p. 243 ff.) feel it necessary with caution to utilize the data in the *Reply to Sadoleto*, I believe it impossible deny its autobiographical accent.
26. John Calvin & Jacopo Sadoleto, *A Reformation Debate, Sadoleto's Letter to the Genevans and Calvin's Reply*. New York, Harper & Row, 1965. p. 84
27 *Ibid.*, pp 84-85
28. Cf. the German original in: *Das Marburger Religionsgespräch* 1529, ed. by Gerhard May, Gutersloh, 1970, pp. 69-70
29. Quoted by Emile Doumergue, *Jean Calvin. Les hommes et les choses de son temps*, Vol. 2, Lausanne, 1902. p. 573
30. One can find this text with Calvin's commentary, the "Brève résolution sur les disputes qui ont été de notre temps quant aux sacrements...," in: *Calvin, homme d'Église*, Geneva, 2nd ed. 1971, pp. 131-191
31. Cf. *op. cit.*, volume 5, Lausanne, 1917, p. 368
32. *Calvin, homme d'Eglise*, p. 141
33. *CO*, vol. XV, col. 212-213
34. *CO*, vol. XVIII, col. 61 f., and Rudolf von Thadden, "Calvin et le progres de la Reforme dans l'Empire," in *La Revue Reformee*, No. 80, 1969/4, p. 18
35. Cf. *Einigungsbestrebungen in der Reformationszeit*, Wiesbaden, 1965
36. Cf. *Ecclesia Reformata. Studies on the Reformation*. Leyden, 1972, p. 113.
37. To the text of the *Invariata: De coena Domini docent, quod corpus et sanguis Christi vere adsint et distribuantur vescentibus in coene Domini*, Melanchthon substituted in the *Variata* the formulation: *De coena Domini docent, quod cum pane et vino vere exhibeantur corpus et sanguis Christi vescentibus in coena Domini*. Cf. *Die Bekenntnisschriften der evangelisch-lutherischen Kirche*, Gottingen, 4th ed. 1959, pp. 64-65.
38. *CO*, vol. XVII, col. 101.
39. *Lettres de Jean Calvin*, ed. by Jules Bonnet, Vol. I, Paris, 1854, pp 420-421.
40. This correspondence was re-edited by Albert-Marie Schmidt under the title *Lettres Anglaises*, Paris, 1959.
41. *Lettres de Jean Calvin*, Vol. 1, p. 269.
42. Cf. *Calvin et l'episcopat. L'episcopat, element organique de l'Eglise dans le calvinisme integral*, Strasbourg, 1927.
43. *CO*, vol. XIV, col. 314.
44. While rejecting the term "hierarchy" which seems "improper" to him, Calvin holds that the institution of the patriarchate is not contrary to Scripture. "If we consider the thing without looking at the word (meaning that of "hierarchy"), we shall find that the ancient bishops had in no wise the intention of forging a form of Church governor, diverse from that form that God has ordained in his Word" (*ICR* IV/IV/4).
45. Cf. *CO*, vol. XV, col. 333.
46. Cf. *Les actes du Concile de Trente, avec le remède contre la poison*, in *Recueil des opuscules, c'est-a-dire petits traites de M. Jean Calvin*, Geneva, 1566, p. 880 ff.

47. *Jules Bonnet, Lettres de Jean Calvin,* vol. 2, Paris, 1854, p. 350, note.

48. *Ibid.,* p. 350-352.

49. Cf. "Réponse à un cauteleux moyenneur qui, sous couleur de pacification, a tâche' de rompre le droit cours de l'Evangile au Royaume de France," in: *Recueil des opuscules,* p. 1912.

50. *CO,* vol. 10b, p. 352ff., and Otto Weber, art. cit., p. 139

51. *Commentaires sur le Nouveau Testament,* Vol. 3, p. 279b.

52. *Ibid.,* p. 319.

53. Cr., Otto Weber, art. cit., p. 139

54. Cf. Martin Schmidt, *A History of the Ecumenical Movement,* ed. by Ruth Rouse and Stephen Charles Neill, London, 1954, pp. 78-79.

55. Cf., art. cit., p. 141.

56. *Die Theologie Calvins,* Munich, 2nd ed. 1957.

57. *Le jeune Calvin. Génèse et évolution de sa vocation réformatrice.* Wiesbaden, 1966, p. 260

58. *Ibid.,* p. 334.

59. In chapter 8 of the third part of the *Smalcald Articles,* the German Reformer writes: "In these sorts of things which are related to the external, oral Word, we must firmly maintain the following principle: God gives to no one his Spirit or grace, other than by or with the external Word which must precede. It is our safeguard against the illuminati or spirituals who flatter themselves as having received the Spirit without or before the Word, and who, in consequence, judge, interpret and falsify the Scripture or the oral Word according to their fantasy. This is that which Müntzer did and which yet today many a person does, who, desiring to fix themselves as judges, distinguish between the spirit and the letter, and know not that which they say or teach. Popery as well, is a pure illuminism, for the Pope affirms that 'all rights are in the casket of his heart' and that all he decides and orders in his Church is spirit and must be held as right, even if this is contrary to Scripture or to the oral Word. All of this comes from the ancient serpent, from the devil who made of Adam and Eve as well illuminati by diverting them from the external Word of God to take them to a false spirituality and to fanciful ideas". Cf. German text in: *Die Bekenntnisschriften der evangelisch-lutherischen Kirche,* pp. 453-454.

60. *A Reformation Debate* . . . pp. 60-61.

Amyraut, Advocate of Reconciliation Between Reformed and Lutherans

There are few periods in the history of Protestant theology so little known as that which extends from the Synod of Dort until the Revocation of the Edict of Nantes (17 October, 1685). Among the theologians of this era, Moise Amyraut, professor at the Academy of Saumur from 1633 until his death in 1664, occupies without doubt one of the loftiest places. A victim of the disgrace into which his century fell, he was not granted the privilege of escaping oblivion despite the works of Jürgen Moltmann, Francois Laplanche and Brian Armstrong [1]. Thus, the name Amyraut no longer means anything for many Protestants, except perhaps, that he was a theoretician of grace, who, for having desired to round off the corners of Calvinistic double predestination, would have created a system called "hypothetical universalism." However, there is in his work a whole series of views which merit attention.

Among the questions worthy of interest, that which Alexander Schweizer considered as the most important [2] has passed nearly unnoticed until now [.3]. We speak here of the efforts attempted by Saumur theologian toward the reconciliation of the Reformed and Lutheran churches. It is to the examination of this question that we now devote ourselves. First, I want to show in what circumstances Amyraut elaborated his "ecumenical" works. Second, I will analyze the doctrine which is expressed in these works.

I

In 1631, the 26th national Synod of the Reformed Churches of France, convened at Charenton, made a decision whose importance history has failed to recognize. Jean Aymon reports it to us in these terms: [4]: "The province of Burgundy having asked if it were permissible for the faithful of the Augsburg Confession to contract their marriages in our churches and to present there as well their children for baptism, without having abjured beforehand the opinions they hold, which are contrary to the beliefs of our Churches? This Synod declares that, because the Churches of the Augsburg Confession agreed with the other reformed Churches in the fundamental points of veritable religion, and had neither superstition nor idolatry in their worship, the faithful of the aforementioned Confession, who in a spirit of friendship and peace, would join themselves to the communion of our churches in this kingdom could, without any recanting, be accepted with us at the table of the Lord"; and, adds David Blondel [5], "to contract marriage with the faithful of our confession," "and that in the capacity of godfathers," pursues Aymon, "they could present children for baptism, provided that they promise the Consistory never to encourage, directly or indirectly, the transgression of the doctrine received and professed in our Churches, but that they instruct and rear them in the points and articles which are common to them and touching that in which the Lutherans and we are in agreement."

This ordinance was to stimulate the highest hopes in the Roman Church. Indeed, through a strange misapprehension, the Catholic theologians imagined that the Reformed, tolerating the Lutheran doctrine of consubstantiation, could also admit transubstantiation such as it had been defined at the Council of Trent [6]. It was necessary to dissipate such an aberration. Jean Daillé [7] and Jean Mestrezat [8] were entrusted by the Church with the defense of the Charenton ordinance. David Blondel refuted Théophile Brachet de la Milletière, Protestant gentleman on the verge of embracing Catholicism, who had accused the 26th national Synod "of having made" with the Lutherans "a hollow peace and a shameful syncretism, from which only disorder will come"[9]. In turn, Moïse Amyraut took up the pen and had published at Saumur, in 1647, after having submitted it-according to the custom of the era- to the ecclesiastical censure [10], a work today extremely rare entitled *De seccessione ab Ecclesia romana deque ratione pacis inter Evangelicos in religionis negotio constituendae disputatio* [11]. As this title indicated, the "ecumenism" of Amyraut fits well in the framework of the apologetic for the Charenton ordinance: for him this problem was, on one hand, to explain the reasons which rendered legitimate the separation with Rome, and, on the other hand, to present the motives which permitted seeking communion with the Churches of the Augsburg Confession.

In his dedication to William VI [12], Landgrave of Hesse, the Saumur theologian explains his position, moreover, in such a fashion as to dissipate any ambiguity. Observing that the partisans of the Pope had not understood the works of his predecessors in defense of the Charenton ordinance, he exposes the two motives that caused him to write: 1) because the Catholics fix their attention on the sole dogma of real presence in the Eucharist, as if that were the unique cause of Protestant secession, Amyraut desires to show that there are, for the churches born of the Reformation, other valid reasons for keeping their distance with Rome (pp. 7-8); 2) because the apologists for the Charenton ordinance, in the advances that they made toward the Lutherans, laid stress in general on the sole problem of the Lord's Supper, he intends to prove that, in other points an understanding is possible with the churches of the Augsburg Confession (p. 9).

A question concerning the *De Secessione:* Why was this work dedicated to a Germanic prince, who, in 1647, was only 18 years of age, and who had not yet taken the reigns of power from his mother? The answer is given us in a passage found in the second "ecumenical" treatise that Amyraut has left us. In the dedicatory Epistle to the Ειρηνικον indeed, the Saumur theologian brings to our attention that William VI had made a trip to France, in 1647, and that he had sojourned at that time for several months on the banks of the Loire, doubtlessly attracted by the reputation of the Academy founded by Philippe du Plessis-Mornay. In his contact with the young prince, Amyraut had appreciated his piety and deemed that he was all but designated for working at the reconciliation of the Protestant churches.

The hopes that the Saumur theologian had put upon the person of William VI were not to be disappointed. Encouraged by the "unionist" efforts of the Lutheran George Calixtus [13], professor at the University of Helmstedt (in the State of Brunswick) and of the Scotsman John Dury [14], who could claim himself as being from all the churches born of the Reformation [15], the Landgrave of Hesse summoned to Cassel, in 1661, a theological colloquy intended to draw the disciples of Luther and Calvin together [16].

To this encounter were invited two representatives of the University of Marburg, then officially Reformed, and two delegates of a Lutheran University today nonexistent, that of Rinteln [17], in the county of Schaumburg. Thus, Sebastian Curtius [18] and John Hein [19] on the Reformed side, and, on the Lutheran side, the disciples of Calixtus, Peter Musaeus [20] and John Henichius [21], were led to consult one another and to underwrite a common declaration on the doctrines of baptism, the person of Christ, predestination and the eucharist [22].

If the Cassel participants were not able to eliminate all divergent points, they were nonetheless under the impression that they had come to agreement on the essential points. As they had decided, in addition, in spite of the questions still under controversy, to consider themselves reciprocally as brothers and members of the true Church of Christ, their decisions had an immense impact. If these decisions provoked the anger of the professors of the Faculty of Wittenberg [23], who believed that Lutheran orthodoxy was threatened, they were on the other hand welcomed joyously in Reformed circles.

Moise Amyraut shared in this enthusiasm. Stimulated by the vast prospects which the Cassel Colloquy seemed to open, conscious of the circulation that the *De secessione* had had in Germany, desirous as well to pursue the work begun at Charenton [24], he felt the need to bring a new contribution to the reconciliatory effort that was beginning within Protestantism. But, as he himself states [25], to all of these reasons was added another, that committed him to this writing. The great-granddaughter of Admiral Gaspard de Coligny, Anne, wife of George II of Wurtemburg, count of Montbéliard, had indeed addressed herself to Amyraut through her chaplain, Jean Melet, former pastor of Sainte Marie-aux-Mines, in order to ask him to express his opinion on the reunification of the Protestants.

Anne de Châtillon was a convinced "unionist"[26], Melet a zelous disciple of John Dury. The Saumur theologian could not shirk their appeal. In rapid fashion, he composed his second "ecumenical treatise"[27], the Ειρηνικον *sive de ratione pacis in religionis negotio inter Evangelicos constutuendae consilium* [28], published in Saumur, in 1662, after having been approved by the Synod of the Churches of Anjou, Touraine and Maine. In order clearly to mark the esteem that he held for the four Cassel theologians, Amyraut dedicated his work to them. With a bit of vanity, he noted in his dedicatory epistle that he must be unknown to them, unless, said he, the renown of the Saumur Academy might have been reflected on his name or that a professorial activity of thirty-five years might have won him some credit.

II

Now that the circumstances motivating the publication of the *De secessione* and the Ειρηνικον have been specified, it is important to bring out the thought contained in these works. Together, one must note at the outset, they constitute an ensemble impressive by its amplitude. Furthermore, in spite of the "sophism," the "subtleties" and the "indefinite argumentation" with which Saigey reproaches them [29], they leave nothing to be desired from the standpoint of clarity. That which one work leaves in the shadows, the other brings to light, so that we can bring out with certainty the profound intention of their author.

One finding becomes immediately noticeable to the one who studies the "ecumenism" of Amyraut: there is not, in his eyes, between the Reformed churches and those of the Augsburg Confession, any impassable obstacle. Calvinists and Lutherans are in agreement on the "fundamental points of veritable religion" (1, pp. 32-33, and 2, p. 341). Together -- this is a grace accorded to them by the Holy Spirit (1, p. 40) -- they find agreement in the explanation of the capital articles of the doctrine whose content has been altered by Rome. In affirming this Amyraut does not tell anything new. He simply picks up and develops the ideas contained in germ form in the Charenton ordinance.

United on the essentials, the Reformed churches and those of the Augsburg Confession are nonetheless separated by numerous divergent points. Certain of these are tolerable. They must be accepted on both sides, for they do not endanger the hope of salvation (2, p. 341).

It is thus, for example -- the absolutism characteristic of the Roman Church being resolutely excluded -- that Amyraut admits, as did Calvin, the legitimacy of diverse ecclesiastical regimes. Next to the egalitarian system of the Reformed churches of France, the Netherlands and Scotland, he accepts the regime of superintendents in operation in the churches of the Augsburg Confession, and even the episcopalism of the Church of England (1, pp. 23-24, and 2, pp. 195-196). He reckons that in imitation of the nations, which are able to federate themselves in spite of different constitutions, the Churches can unite in spite of the diversity of their regimes (1, pp. 27-28).

In the category of acceptable divergent points, one must again classify those which have rites as their origin. While being a partisan of simplicity in the worship service which he feels originates with the apostles themselves, the Saumur theologian shows himself ready to allow in the Lutheran Church images, candles, the sign of the cross at the administration of baptism, and kneeling on reception of the Eucharistic elements (1, pp. 226-236, and 2, pp. 341-348). What is important for Amyraut - he declares it in the *De secessione* on the subject of bap-tism and the Lord's Supper - is that each Church conserve its manner of doing things without wanting to impose it upon the other, and that, if one of the faithful is called upon to attend the services of the sister denomination, he do so in conformity with the customs in force (1, pp. 231-232).

But, as we have already alluded, there is a second category of divergent points between Calvinists and Lutherans. This category involves five specific dogmas : those of baptism, the Lord's Supper, the person of Christ, predestination and providence (1, pp. 63-64, and 2, pp. 197-198). On each of these points, Amyraut feels, the Reformed churches and those of the Augsburg Confession agree on the essen-tials. But on each of these as well, they are separated by a certain num-ber of contested points which are not inconsequential. It is therefore to reduce these divergent points, or if this reduction is not possible, to show that these differences are tolerable, that the Saumur theologian is now to apply himself.

Before dealing with the first of these controversial questions, the question of baptism [30], Amyraut, in the *De secessione*, dedicates an entire exposition to the doctrine of the sacrament in general. After having brought out the agreement which exists between Reformed and Lutherans with respect to the Roman Church - both, indeed, reject the doctrine of the *ex opere operato* and recognize as sacramental acts only baptism and the Lord's Supper (1, pp. 65-66) - he notes two subjects of controversy:

1. Contrary to the members of the churches of the Augsburg Con-fession who judge that the Old Covenant is not of the same essence as the New, the disciples of Calvin tend to attribute to the sacraments of the old Covenant the same value as those of the New. This is the dif-ference of little importance in the eyes of the Saumur theologian, since both deem that, until the epiphany of Christ, the sacraments of the Old Covenant procured for believers the remission of sins and the gift of the Holy Spirit (1, pp. 67-69)!

2. While, for the Reformed, the sacraments and the preaching of the

Word operate in the same manner, the Lutherans hold that, without being able to explicate its precise nature, there is in baptism and the Lord's Supper an element which does not exist in preaching. Here again, the controversy holds no interest for Amyraut. It is enough for him to say that, pertaining to efficacy, the sacraments and the preaching of the Word have numerous things in common (1, pp. 70-73).

But let us now come to baptism and here follow the Ειρηνικον whose thought is infinitely more subtle and more developed than that of the *De secessione* [31]. With a precision a bit too scholastic, the Saumur theologian feels that this sacrament raises difficulties by reason of the manner in which Lutherans and Calvinists conceive of its power, its necessity, its administration and its rite of observation. We shall not take time to bring out all the details of this text. We will limit ourselves to developing its principal aspects.

On the power of baptism (2, pp. 208-212), Amyraut points out two subjects of dispute. On the one hand, the Lutherans hold that through this sacrament the children of believers are introduced into God's Covenant, while for the Reformed, children born of Christian parents must be baptized because they are born into this Covenant. On the other hand, the Lutherans affirm that baptism produces a certain kind of faith in the nursling, while for the Reformed, the infant is incapable of believing.

The first of these two difficulties is resolved easily by the Saumur theologian. He shows that the birth into the church signified by baptism in the eyes of certain Lutherans - he quotes here John Gerhard [32] - implies as an after-effect a birth within the Covenant. As for the second contestable point, Amyraut disposes of it with equal facility. The Reformed, he says, can tolerate the Lutheran assertion in which baptism administered to the infant creates faith in him, for we cannot assign a limit to the action of the Holy Spirit.

The person of the one administering baptism brings out another point of contention (2, pp. 216-218). The Lutherans hold that it ordinarily belongs to the minister of the gospel to baptize, but also to any private person in extraordinary cases. The Reformed feel, on the other hand, that there is no necessity that would obligate an adult or a child to be baptized by anyone other than a regularly-ordained pastor.

While bringing out that the theologians of the Augsburg Confession do not see in baptism, as does the Roman Church, the *sine qua non* of salvation, Amyraut remarks that this sacrament has nonetheless for them a necessitous character such that in order to obtain it, one can "transgress" ecclesiastical order. It is therefore an objection of an ecclesiological nature that the author of the Ειρηνικον raises against the Lutheran practice. That laymen might baptize, even in exceptional cases, is a fact which does not correspond to his notion of the ministry. He is, however, disposed to tolerate it in Christian charity, for it prejudices neither the hope of salvation nor the purity of worship.

The baptismal rite constitutes a last subject of controversy between the Reformed and the Lutherans, the gravest of all in Amyraut's judgement (2, pp. 218-220). The Saumur theologian here stands against the exorcism which exists at that period in the liturgies of the churches of the Augsburg Confession. To him it is a formula which has no correspondence in Lutheran dogma, and much more; it is also a custom that is vain and unworthy of the Christian religion. It is horrifying to him to think that children born of Christian parents could be considered comparable to pagans, who, rightly so, were asked formerly to renounce Satan. Also, as Sebastian Curtius and John Hein at the Cassel Colloquy had done [33], Amyraut invites the Lutherans purely and simply to remove this exorcism.

★

The second question which is the object of controversy between Calvinists and Lutherans is that of the eucharist [34]. As Amyraut notes, it was originally the sole subject of dispute between the Reformers; but in and of itself, it is sufficiently important for explaining the division of Protestants (2, pp. 220).

One must not think, however, that there is no agreement on this question between the Reformed churches and those of the Augsburg Confession. In opposition to Rome, they both rejected, as the *De secessione* notes (pp. 79-83), transubstantiation, the sacrifice of the mass, communion in one element, private masses, and the adoration of the sacrament. But the agreement goes yet deeper. Indeed, if, at the Marburg Colloquy, Luther and Zwingli were unable to agree on the manner in which Christ was present in the Lord's Supper, they nevertheless reached the same conclusions on all other aspects of eucharistic dogma. Even more, they decided then to keep within the family the only divergence that manifested itself between them (1, pp. 119-120).

In this connection, the Saumur theologian quotes the end of the 15th and last article of the declaration signed by Luther and Zwingli at the end of their negotiations. We bring this to remembrance, because the Marburg Colloquy has become a synonym for disunion and acrimony. "Though we would not be presently in agreement on the question (of knowing) whether the true body and blood of the Lord are corporally present in the bread and the wine of the Supper, however each party will bear witness to the Christian charity of the other, as much as his conscience is able, and both will pray ardently to God to guide us into the true doctrine by his Spirit".

Having said this, let us look, according to the *De secessione* in particular - as to this question, the Ειρηνικον takes a backward step in comparison to the 1647 writing [35] - at how, on the subject of the Supper, Amyraut catches sight of the possibility of a reconciliation between Calvinists and Lutherans.

If the former believe that, in the eucharist, Christ is present in a mystical or sacramental manner (1, pp. 87-94, and 2, pp. 253-258), the latter hold, on the contrary, that the body of the Lord is found "in," "with" and "under" the two elements in a fashion that surpasses the sacramental reality of the Reformed position and that one might be tempted to call "substantial" (1, pp. 94-95). This divergence, already considerable, is aggravated by certain Lutheran theologians who think that in virtue of the *communicatio idiomatum* the body of Christ exists in every place (1, p. 95 and 2, pp. 271-273). Of recent origin and of an inspiration foreign to Luther (Amyraut commits here an error) [36], this doctrine of ubiquity - contradicted according to our author by the fact that, since the Ascension, Christ possesses a glorified body -is the cause of gravest misunderstanding. By denying that God would permit a body to be everywhere present at once (1, p. 96), the Reformed see themselves accused by the Lutherans of stripping the Supper of its most sacred aspect. On the other hand, by attributing to Christ a body which is not circumscribed in space (1, p. 97) the Lutherans are suspected by the Reformed of rejecting the human nature of the Saviour.

In what manner is the author of the *De secessione* to resolve the difficulty, which, one must admit, is not lacking in gravity? By distinguishing very subtly between the arguments of theologians and the essential elements of religion. These elements are two in number: the worship service and the declaration of faith (1, p. 102). Now, Amyraut feels, the Lutheran worship service has not been contaminated by the doctrine of ubiquity (1, pp. 102-103). As for the Augsburg Confession, it limits itself to the affirmation that the body and blood of Christ are truly present under the elements of the bread and the wine [37]. It does not attempt to qualify the mode of this presence. It shows proof of the "prudence" and "modesty" that the Council of Trent did not manifest when it defined the dogma of transubstantiation (1, pp. 103-104).

Thus, since the Lutheran worship service and the Augsburg Confession do not contain, relative to the eucharist, any element that the Calvinists could not accept; since, in addition, the Lutherans are obligated to recognize that the Reformed doctrine of the Supper is scriptural, and that at the most it sins by default, in not including all that the Scriptures teach with respect to the sacraments (2, pp. 221-222), Amyraut holds that intercommunion is possible between the Reformed churches and those of the Augsburg Confession [38]. Both parties being in agreement on the essential elements of eucharistic dogma, their duty is mutually to accept one another without seeking to hide their own particular opinions on the subject.

Here is what Amyraut declares about this in the Ειρηνικον : "Assuredly, we would very much desire to convince the Lutherans, because we believe that our doctrine is true, in conformity with Scripture and with religion. But, if we can obtain nothing from them, we acquiesce in their keeping of their opinions; we will tolerate them in good grace, for we hold that they contain no pernicious poison. On their side, let the Lutherans attempt to win us to their ideas if they can ! For they are persuaded that these are absolutely pure and authentic. Nonetheless, because we are of another opinion than they as to the presence of the body of Christ, we ask them that they require of us no abjuration of our dogma, but that they allow us to adhere openly to it ... Our desire is that the Lutherans not refuse to take the Supper in our churches, since we in no way obligate them to abjure, and, even, that they permit us to take communion with them, without requiring of us that we renounce our doctrine (pp. 277-278).

Amyraut does not limit himself to proposing intercommunion between the Reformed churches and those of the Augsburg Confession. Extending the perspectives opened by the Charenton ordinance, he proposes in the *De secessione* that Calvinists and Lutherans together compose a declaration of faith in which they will express the views that they hold in common on the question of the eucharist. The mode of Christ's presence in the elements will there be qualified by the adverbs *realiter* and *sacramentaliter* [39]. The interpretation of these two words will be permitted to each of the two confessions, on the condition that, in private discussions, in the sermons and in theological writings, all controversies be renounced that can injure fraternal concord.

Christology [40] brings out a third contested point between Reformed and Lutherans, which must not make them forget all that they have in common in this area. Indeed, they both allow that Christ is true God from all eternity, that the person of the Son is distinct from that of the Father from before all ages, that the Son incarnated himself, becoming like ourselves in all things, save sin, and finally, that the human nature of Christ began to exist only at the moment of its union with the Logos (1, pp. 127-130, and 2, pp. 280-282).

But it is not only to this that the agreement existing between the Reformed churches and those of the Augsburg Confession is limited. As Amyraut brings out in the Ειρηνικον (pp. 282-285), the disciples of Calvin accept with those of Luther the Christological dogma as formulated by the Chalcedon Council; they believe that the two natures of Christ are united without being confused [41], without the one being converted into the other [42], without one being finally able to separate them or to divide them [43]. But the Reformed go even further: they share with the Lutherans the ideas of the ancient fathers on the *communicatio idiomatum*. They thus think that the attributes of one of the natures can be transferred to the entire person of Christ, that that which applies to Christ in the integrality of his person can be said at times of one or the other of his natures, that that which is in harmony with one of the natures can sometimes be attributed to the other, without, however, confusing the two natures or mixing their properties (1, pp. 136-138 and 2, pp. 285-287).

If such is the case, what is the nature of disagreement which sets the Reformed churches and those of the Augsburg Confession in opposition? The following fact: while the Calvinists, desiring to highlight the significance of the Ascension, look to heaven for the humanity of Christ, without forgetting, however, that in virtue of his divinity the glorified Lord is omnipresent (2, pp. 287-290), the Lutherans, certain ones at least, hold that in virtue of the hypostatic union, the body of Christ is endowed with ubiquity in the same manner as his divine nature (2, p. 294). This omnipresence of Christ's body, of which we have already spoken in reference to the eucharist, is dangerous in Amyraut's eyes, because it introduces confusion in the union of the two natures: it permits one wrongly to suppose that the body of Christ was stripped of all humanity (2, p. 296).

How can this stalemate be broken? The Saumur theologian feels first of all, that in this problem, the two confronting parties must abstain from drawing from their adversaries' systems conclusions that would be disapproved by the latter. Thus, let not the Reformed accuse their interlocutors of following Eutyches and of sinking into monophysitism! The Lutherans, indeed, do not deny the humanity of the body of Christ, they do not assert that the human nature has been abolished in the Saviour's person, they do not teach that the glorified Lord is foreign to men. And, on their side, let not the Lutherans accuse those who refuse to admit the ubiquity of the body of Christ of being disciples of Nestorius! The Reformed, indeed, affirm strongly the unity of the person of the Incarnate Word (1, p. 139, and 2, p. 297).

These misunderstandings dismissed, the problem for Amyraut is summarized in this: the partisans of ubiquity feel, on one hand, that Christ took on a truly human body, and that, on the other hand, the human body taken on by Christ is everywhere. In the eyes of the Saumur theologian, there are here two contradictory propositions (2, p. 297). Let the Reformed tolerate this contradiction! And let the Lutherans, on their side, allow that the Calvinists do not draw from the *communicatio idiomatum* all that they themselves believe to infer from it (2, pp. 290-291).

Amyraut- it is here that he reveals a true theologian's temperament -does not content himself, however, with this invitation to mutual tolerance. In the *De Secessione,* he proposes that Reformed and Lutherans adhere to a common Christological declaration. The essential elements of it would be the following: Christ is God, Christ is man, Christ is at once God and man. Christ is a unique being. There is in him but one hypostasis, that which, in an incomprehensible manner, was communicated to the human nature by the eternal Word. In the person of Christ as well, there are two natures, united in such a way that they do not constitute two hypostases; two natures which, in spite of their union, are not confused; two natures, finally, whose different properties are communicated among themselves in such a fashion as to effectuate, together and not separably, our salvation (1, pp. 148-149).

Having thus resolved the problem of the ubiquity of the body of Christ and held that should the controversies relative to it not cease, one should relegate them to the theological schools where they should be handled with the greatest moderation possible (1, p. 149), Amyraut again brings out in the *De Secessione* a point of disagreement among the Reformed and the Lutherans. It is that of the sufferings that Christ underwent in his soul before dying. Following Calvin, the Reformed think that the agonies of the Saviour at Calvary are due to the fact that he carried the weight of our sins. The Lutherans, on the other hand, feel it injurious to Christ to hold that he trembled before the justice of God and that by experiencing dread, he came to know the penalty of the damned (1, pp. 150-151).

Amyraut has no trouble disposing of this disputed point, a secondary one besides. Bringing out that, in the Gospels, the Passion includes physical sufferings and spiritual torments, he does not hesitate in believing that Reformed and Lutherans will be able to subscribe to a common declaration which will express in all its tragedy the expiatory sacrifice of the Son of God (1, pp. 154-156).

After having disposed of the baptismal, eucharistic and Christological controversies for which the Lutherans are responsible by virtue of certain particularities of their teaching, Amyraut attempts to resolve the difficulties that are created for the churches of the Augsburg Confession by the Reformed doctrines of predestination [44] and providence.

Let us look, first, at that which is related to predestination! In this area, as in the others, the Reformed and the Lutherans have numerous points in common. Thus, they recognize together that the fall corrupted the human faculties "of which one may have some need in the area of religion," as Amyraut declares with prudence in the *De Secessione* (p. 157), avoiding to speak of a total corruption of man. The Reformed churches and those of the Augsburg Confession agree, in addition, in thinking that faith is a gift of God. Unscathed by Pelagianism, they are at last pure from any Manicheism. If they recognise the action of the Holy Spirit in the heart of the believer, they know also that this action implies neither ignorance nor inertia on man's part.

These convergent points noted, Amyraut presents thus the principal controversy which puts Reformed and Lutherans in opposition on the point of predestination. While the former hold that the expiatory work of Christ is not in any manner valid for those who do not benefit from election, the latter affirm that this work is valid for the nonelect in a certain manner, that is, *sub conditione fidei* (1, p. 166). The shade of meaning appears to us today as being extremely subtle. In order to render the problem more accessible let us say that to the *gratia objectiva* of the Reformed (that grace which consists of the preaching of the Gospel to all men without distinction, to the elect as to the non-elect), the Lutherans add, contrary to the Calvinists, for whom subjective grace is reserved to the few, a *gratia communis interior* (in virtue of which, with the proclamation of salvation, would be offered to each one, the possibility of believing (2, pp. 300-301).

To resolve this difficulty, Amyraut brings out first that the *gratia communis interior* of the Lutherns which others call "sufficient" (2, p. 301) or "efficacious" (2, p. 307), is not really such. It confers the gift of "being able to believe" and not that of "believing." This reservation stated, the Saumur theologian recalls that, for Calvin, the sacrifice of Christ is capable of redeeming all men, and that to all salvation is truly offered whenever the Word of God is preached (2, pp. 302-304). But Amyraut does not stop there. After having shown that, for the author of the *Institutes of the Christian Religion*, the doctrine of election has the goal of exalting the glory of God and of delivering man from fear by rendering his salvation independent of his own miserable resources (2, pp. 301-302), he quotes one of the canons of the Synod of Dort, to which the French Reformed felt tied by the decision of the Alès Synod (1620) [45].

Here is this text, which expresses in excellent terms the extensiveness which the Calvinists attribute to objective grace: "All those who are called by the Gospel are called efficaciously: for God declares very seriously and veritably by His Word that which is pleasing to Him, to wit, that all those who are called come to Him, and this is why He promises very seriously that all those who come and believe in Him will find rest for their soul and will have eternal life"[46].

Calvin and Dort! These two witnesses quoted in favor of his Reformed orthodoxy, Amyraut moves all the more easily to the point of encounter with the Lutherans in that his hypothetical universalism inclined him in this direction. Without renouncing the idea of making subjective grace (that grace which, from the possibility of faith, leads to faith) the privilege of the sole elect, he attributes to the objective grace of the Calvinists all the characteristics of the *gratia communis interior* dear to the Lutherans. To preaching, which is addressed to all men, God would add in this manner, for all men equally, the illumination which would permit them to believe (1, pp. 181-185, and 2, pp. 305-307).

It is necessary here to digress in order to bring out in what manner Amyraut's concession relative to objective grace has been judged. In his *Histoire des variations des Églises protestantes*, Bossuet imagined that the "call" and the "universal grace" taught by the school of Saumur originated from the "indulgence that they had there for the Lutherans"[47]. This is a gratuitous supposition. The treatise *De la prédestination* (1634) is, indeed thirteen years earlier than the *De secessione*. Moreover, the need to render explicit the thought of Calvin on the problem of election made itself felt well before the birth of Amyraldian "ecumenism." It is, therefore, not by desire to reconcile the Reformed churches and those of the Augsburg Confession that Amyraut embraced hypothetical universalism. It is, on the contrary, after having elaborated this doctrine that he discovered the role that it could play in dialogue with the Lutherans [48].

But let us return to the disagreements brought out between Reformed and Lutherans by the doctrine of predestination. Amyraut notes that the members of the churches of the Augsburg Confession, counter to the Calvinists, do not want to hear of "absolute decrees." the Saumur theologian responds to this difficulty - he thinks that the Lutherans will fall in line with his opinion - that the election decree is "absolute" because it depends on the sole will of God, nothing in man being worthy of receiving faith and of meriting salvation. As for the decree of reprobation, it also possesses this same character of absoluteness, for if the rejected are worthy of being forgotten by grace, they are however, not more unworthy than the elect (1, pp. 172-181, and 2, pp. 307-309).

According to the Ειρηνικον (pp. 309-313), the Lutherans still reproach the Reformed doctrine of predestination as containing a certain fatalism. The objection is dismissed easily, too easily, by Amyraut. Why, he says, choose to call "fatal" God's secret purpose? Why not look for, more simply, the cause of election in the faith of the believer, the origin of reprobation in the unbelief of the wicked?

These answers being taken for what they are - they belong more to parenetics than to dogmatics! - let us look, finally, as does the *De secessione,* at a last difficulty created by the Calvinistic conception of predestination: that of the perseverance of the saints (1, pp. 185-187). The Reformed affirm that true faith cannot cease to exist. The Lutherans, on the other hand, think that this faith can die away in order to be reborn. The debate holds little importance in the eyes of Amyraut. He feels the one and the other are in agreement, since they are in agreement, since they are equally convinced that those who once believed truly cannot fail to receive salvation [49].

The doctrine of providence [50] is a fifth and last item of contention between Reformed and Lutherans. Here again, however, points of agreement are not lacking. As *De secessione* brings out, both admit that God has foreseen the course of things from all eternity, that he has decided to supply everything, and that in his providence he resorts to the use of secondary causes. Both, hold, finally, that there is no *fatum,* neither in good, nor in evil (pp. 192-197).

What, therefore is the nature of the misunderstanding which, on this question, separates the churches born out of Reformation? It is that the Lutherans accuse the Calvinists, in spite of their denials and their protestations of innocence, of considering God as the author of sin (1, pp. 205-206 and 2, pp. 313-314).

It is to refute this accusation that Amyraut now turns his attention. He notes, first, that providence can use evil; this then becomes for the man who is struck by evil, either the punishment for his sin, or again a call to repentance, or finally an invitation to bear more fruit (2, pp. 315-316). But the Saumur theologian goes further. In a series of infinitely subtle expositions, where he abuses Aristotle's categories (2, p. 325), he intends to show that, if God is not the cause of evil, providence nonetheless exercises toward sin an action which is more than permissive [51]. Taking up in this vein the story of the passion, he points out that God caused the good of humanity to result from the avarice of Judas, from the hatred of the leaders of Israel, from the cruelty of the crowd and from the cowardice of Pilate (1, pp. 197-198, and 2, pp. 323-324).

The Amyraldian thought is clear: not to hinder an action from taking place is not really to command it. To say of providence that it only permits evil is to not acknowledge its power of government. It is necessary, therefore, to add to the permissive action of providence a factor in virtue of which God conducts the events inspired by sin, and by sin alone, in such a manner that they contribute finally to his glory, to the good of humanity and to the salvation of his church. (2, pp. 338-339).

Persuaded that the accusation of the Lutherans against the Reformed doctrine of providence collapses under the heavy blows of his argument, Amyraut proposes in the *De secessione* a declaration which could be acceptable to the Calvinists and to the members of the churches of the Augsburg Confession. It proclaims that the universe is governed by providence, this government implying not only that God makes himself obeyed, but also that he directs everything by his hand, without being thereby the author of evil (1, p. 206).

After having disposed of the divergent points caused by baptism, the Supper, Christology, predestination and providence, Amyraut holds that nothing can any longer hinder the Reformed churches and those of the Augsburg Confession from concluding an accord pleasing to God. With the purpose of preparing this reconciliation, he proposes at the end of the *De secessione*, but especially in the last chapter of the Ειρηνικον (which, by itself, constitutes a veritable treatise of more than sixty pages), a series of measures [52] which still merit our attention.

It is necessary first, Amyraut feels, that discussion be established between Reformed and Lutherans. To this effect, it will be good to organize encounters which will bring together theologians of both churches. In the course of the exchanges that will take place then, both will learn to appreciate each other; as a result, they will abandon their reciprocal prejudices and will cease mutually considering themselves as monsters (2, pp. 352-353).

In order that these encounters be fruitful, Amyraut thinks that three precautions must be taken. It will first be necessary, if one intends to establish a lasting concord, that the love of truth surpass the desire to triumph. It will then be necessary to avoid evaluating the truth on the basis of a vote organized among the participants, for, either the votes will be equally divided between Reformed and Lutherans (and, in this case, the discussions will never terminate), or the representatives of one of the denominations fewer in number that those of the sister church will be defeated (and, in this case the vanquished will feel oppressed along with the truth that they are defending). It will be necessary, finally, to avoid blending contrary opinions, for such admixtures result in ambiquous declarations which are the cause of new controversies (2, pp. 353-359).

After having given these three pieces of advice, whose pertinence and current application we cannot emphasize sufficiently, Amyraut cites the Council of Trent as an example of a poor compromise and the Cassel Colloquy as a model of happy reconciliation. The Council of Trent, indeed, in desiring to maintain a certain balance in the doctrine of grace, which was the object of controversy among its participants, only succeeded in preparing the Jansenist crisis (2, p. 359). The Cassel Colloquy, on the other hand, was able to lay the foundation of an authentic and lasting concord.

We will not be cruel enough to counter Amyraut's judgement on this last point with the denial that history has inflicted upon him. It appears more interesting to us to know the reasons why the encounter between the theologians of Marburg and Rinteln takes on such a great importance in his eyes. It is, first of all, because the Cassel interlocutors, after having distinguished the fundamental points of the faith, saw that Reformed and Lutherans agree upon them. It is also because Curtius and Hein, Musaeus and Henichius, did not seek to disguise their dissensions and elaborate a dubious mixture of opinions, but concerning each contested doctrine, they brought out the limits of their disagreement to establish the fact that they could tolerate their differences. It is, finally, because the theologians summoned by William VI deliberately put aside all nonessential problems, which should not constitute an obstacle to Christian unity (2, pp. 360-362).

But the discussions between Reformed and Lutherans must not only take place in the framework of a few encounters. They must be pursued as well in epistolary exchanges which Amyraut feels more useful, in certain ways, than oral conversations. A letter, indeed, can go everywhere (which was not the case of the Reformed theologians of France who did not then have the authorization to cross the borders of the Kingdom!). A letter, in addition, is generally more moderate, more precise than an oral intervention. All these are reasons why the Saumur theologian, who appears wary of oratorical tilting, favors dialogues which develop via the pen! He does not, however, underrate the dangers of the epistolary style. He recommends avoiding the endless polemics in the course of which the printers' presses are no longer able to suffice. He advises setting aside the violence and the harshness to which Luther and Calvin, "these two lights of the Christian Church," at times abandoned themselves. (2, pp. 362-367, 372-373 and 377-378).

To these warnings Amyraut adds, still in regard to epistolary exchanges, a series of recommendations which appear valid to us in the wider field of any ecumenical confrontation. He thus invites the theologians always to present positively the thought of their interlocutors, always to deduce from the system of their adversaries only those conclusions admitted to by the latter, finally, always to judge the doctrine of a church only after the public documents of its faith, to wit, its declaration of faith, its liturgy and its catechism (2, pp. 367-371).

After these suggestions, designed to make of the exchanges between Reformed and Lutherans genuine occasions for encounter, the Saumur theologian sets forth the duties of the faithful, the pastors, the synods and the princes desirous of working toward the reconciliation of the Protestants.

As Amyraut says in the *De secessione*, it belongs to the faithful to assist the efforts of the pastors and to support the "unionist" decisions of the princes "through vows, prayers, fasts, tears, holy thoughts and pious stirrings of the souls" (p. 268). The Ειρηνικον expects also of the faithful that, once that concord is re-established, they do not seek, if they are called upon to live in a sister church, to question its doctrine (p. 383).

The pastors receive a serious warning. Considering that between those of the Reformed churches and those who adhere to the Augsburg Confession there is a greater gap than that which exists among their respective flocks, the Saumur theologian admonishes them to show proof of "prudence", of "moderation" and of "charity" (1, pp. 249-250 and 266-268). In their sermons, they will avoid taking up controversial subjects. Indeed, there are in Scripture enough passages on which the two churches are in accord with which they can content themselves (1, pp. 237-242 and 245-246). But Amyraut sees further. Waiting for the era when, reconciliation made, the pastors will be able to serve indifferently one or the other of the churches (1, pp. 262-263), he feels, that it would be not only useful, but necessary that Reformed and Lutheran ministers address themselves on occasion to the congregations of the sister denomination (2, p. 387).

The roles of the faithful and the pastors thus specified, the author of the Εἰρηνικόν sets down that of the synods [53]. Noting that it is yet impossible to bring together Reformed and Lutherans in one single synod, he desires that the synods of both denominations exchange delegates, who will not only be welcomed with deference and kindness, but who will as well receive the right of vote in all questions foreign to denominational controversies. Beside this desire, Amyraut expects the Reformed and Lutheran synods to elect men entrusted with the task of laying the theological foundations of a future reconciliation. In the course of the discussions held by these official representatives, any attempt at proselytism will be banished. If, however, a conversation should take place on one side or the other, it should be openly recognized that each person is free to follow the injunctions of his conscience; it should even be agreed - Amyraut goes this far - that the pastor, who, won over by the arguments of his interlocutors would adhere to their denomination, be able to remain in his parish in case that the latter's desire be such. There is finally, a last measure that the Reformed and Lutheran Synods should adopt. As numerous problems come before them in identical terms, it is necessary, even before they attain to unity, that they create common organisms in order to resolve them (2, pp. 392-395).

As for the duty of princes, it is of considerable importance. It is on them, indeed - the Elector of Saxony, the Palatine Elector, the Landgrave of Hesse and the Duke of Würtemburg - that, in Εἰρηνικόν [54] Amyraut makes the success of the Protestant reunification depend. Their task will be to invite the theologians to engross themselves with the problem of unity; to organize colloquies which, if possible, they will attend to give them more weight; to bring about "unionist" writings in the common tongues in order to have the people participate in the reconciliation of the sons of the Reformation; to convoke the synod which will restore concord among Protestants; to bring together perhaps the evangelical churches into one sole body, removing thus a schism which is an obstacle to the propagation of truth and an offense against the glory of God (pp. 395-402).

Having come to the end of our analysis, we could attack the manner in which Amyraut sometimes resolved the divergent points between Calvinists and Lutherans [55], and bring out certain weaknesses in the means that he proposes toward the goal of reconciling the Protestants [56]. It appears to us more fair, however, to conclude this chapter by bringing out all that is prophetic in the "ecumenism" of the Saumur theologian.

Here again, of course, we could discuss his conception of Christian unity, which presents a certain analogy to the "branch theory" dear to certain Anglican theologians [57]. We could bring out as well the limits that he assigns to fraternal concord from which he excludes the Roman Church, not without sorrow, it is true (2, pp. 350-351). But these reservations would be too simple, and vain as well, for, as everyone knows, the theology of ecumenism is today but at the point of its first faltering words.

Rather than a critique, then, it is a frank admiration for their author that the *De secessione* and the Ειρηνικον inspire in us. These two works reveal to us a believer and a theologian. A believer who, while being faithfully attached to his church, desired the *Una sancta* with all his soul. A theologian who knew that unity does not come about by means of simple effusions, but in the harsh search for the truth [58].

Would Amyraut's "ecumenism" not have left some trace in history? This question, which we must put in closing, we believe can be answered affirmatively, while reserving the right to lend support to our judgement on another occasion. It will suffice to bring out here that the English Quaker who was the governor and legislator of Pennsylvania, William Penn, left the University of Oxford to continue his studies at Saumur, where, between 1661 and 1664, he was the student and perhaps even the guest of Moise Amyraut [59]. 1661, this is the date of the Cassel Colloquy; 1662, that of the publication of the Ειρηνικον. It is not impossible to think that Penn was one of the witnesses of the composition of this work. It is especially permissible to feel that the Amyraldian views on the reconciliation of the Protestants had a part in inspiring the Quaker statesman's love of concord [60].

If such is the case, we cannot form the rather pungent conclusion that the "ecumenical" heritage of Amyraut, modified in the direction of a certain doctrinal indifference, become through the mediation of William Penn the attribute of the Society of Friends. But we must not rest contentedly with this surprising conclusion. Having become aware that Amyraldian irenism was ignored for several centuries, we need to be conscious of its current application: it has doubtless a current instruction for those Reformed and Lutherans anxious to affirm, beyond their divergences, the truth common to the Churches born in the spiritual renewal in the sixteenth century.

Notes

1. Cf. respectively "Prädestination und Heilsgeschichte bei Moyse Amyraut. Ein Beitrag zur Geschichte der reformierten Theologie zwischen Orthodoxie und Aufklärung", in: *Zeitschrift für Kirchengeschichte,* vol. 65, Stuttgart, 1953/1954, pp. 270-303; *Orthodoxie et Predication. L'Oeuvre D'Amyraut et la querelle de la grâce universelle,* Paris, 1965: and Brian G. Armstrong, *Calvinism and the Amyraut Heresy, Protestant Scholasticism and Humanism in Seventeenth Century France,* Madison, Wisconsin, 1969.

2. Cf. his article on Amyraut in the *Realencyklopädie für protestantische Theologie und Kirche,* 3rd ed., vol. 1, Leipzig, 1896, p. 479.

3. Only Alexander Schweizer perceived this important aspect of Amyraldian thought to which he reserved a paragraph in his work *Die protestantischen Centraldogmen in ihrer Entwicklung innerhalb der reformierten Kirche,* vol., 2, Zurich, 1856, pp. 505-517. The Zurich theologian's study presents however three fundamental flaws: 1. it is but partial and neglects all that which, in Amyraut's "ecumenism", is foreign to the "central dogmas of Protestantism" (the doctrines of predestination and providence); 2. it consists of a list of quotations, often truncated, juxtaposed in an order foreign to the author's thought; 3. it is based on only one of the works which will be treated below, the Ειρηνικον, disregarding completely the *De secessione.*

4. In *Actes ecclésiastiques et civils de tous les synodes nationaux des Églises Réformées de France,* vol. 2, La Haye, 1710, pp. 500-501, Article I of chapter XXII.

5. Beside this adjunction, the text of the Charenton ordinance that Blondel gives us is identical in its basis to that which we find in Aymon's work. As to the formulation, it is different in the one and the other of our two sources; this phenomenon should not surprise us: in the manner of quotations, one did not have in the XVIIth century the same rigor as is the case today. Cf. David Blondel, *Actes authentiques des Églises réformées de France, Germanie, Grande-Bretagne, Pologne, Hongrie, Païs-Bas, etc. Touchant la paix et charite' fraternelle que tous les serviteurs de Dieu doivent sainctement entretenir avec les protestants qui ont quelque diversité, soit d'expression, soit de méthode, soit mesme de sentiment . . .,* Amsterdam, 1655, p. 8.

6. Elie Benoist writes to this effect in his *Histoire de L' Édit de Nantes...* (vo. 2, Delft, 1693): "The missionaries thought all obstacles to reunification with the Roman Church lifted by this declaration; because they did not conceive that the Reformed had to have more repugnance for the Transubstantiation of the Catholics than for the Impanation and Ubiquity of the Lutherans; principally since the Synod recognized that in the latter's doctrine, even if there were error, there was no venom; and that in their worship there was no idolatry" (p. 525).

7. Cf. David Blondel, *Actes authentiques des Églises réformées... touchant la paix et charite' fraternelle,* p. 9.

8. Cf. Ernst Ludwig Theodor Henke, *Georg Calixtus und seine Zeit,* vol. II/1, Marburg, 1856, p. 160.

9. David Blondel, *op. cit.,* p. 9.

10. The *De secessione* (cf. p. 286) was read and approved by the pastors of the church of Baugé (colloquy of Anjou) and of L'Ile-Bouchard (colloquy of Touraine).

11. This book was re-edited in Germany, probably several years after its publication in France. It will be designated in the text of this lecture by the number: 1.

12. Fifth child of the Landgrave William V, William VI was born in Cassel in 1629, died at Haina (Hesse) in 1663. After the death of his father, in 1637, his mother, Amelia Elisabeth, born Countess of Hanau, assumed the regency until 1650. During his 13-year reign, William VI worked above all for the strengthening of the faith and for the development of education, as well as for the increase of well-being for his people. His activity merited him, and rightly so, the nickname of "the Just". Cf. *Allgemeine deutsche Biographie*, vol. 43, Leipzig, 1898, pp. 54-60. On the place occupied by the reign of William VI in the history of Hesse, cf. Karl E. Demandt, *Geschichte des Landes Hessen*, Cassel and Basel, 1959, pp. 199-200.

13. Born in 1586, Calixtus was professor at the University of Helmstedt from 1614 until his death, in 1656. Heir to the conciliatory ideal dear to Melanchthon, he underwent during his career very strong attacks from "orthodox" Lutherans (among them, Abraham Calov) who reproached him for his "syncretism."

14. Born in 1595, Dury, after several years of pastoral ministry, dedicated his life, from 1628 to his death in 1680, to the desire for reconciling the various churches born of the Reformation. In 1655, he was recommended to William VI by Cromwell, who desired to unite the Protestant world under the shield of England. A few years later, he established himself at Cassel from where he maintained, in the service of his ideal, an extended correspondence with the princes, the cities, the universities and the churches of Reformed Christianity.

15. Norman Sykes writes to this effect in *A History of the Ecumenical Movement* (ed. by Ruth Rouse and Stephen Charles Neill, London, 1954): "His career (implying that of Dury) indeed was so ecumenical, or cosmopolitan, that it is difficult to decide to which Church and country his religious biography properly belongs, whilst his ecclesiastical allegiance defies definition; for he received first Presbyterian ordination by the Presbytery at Dort; then Anglican ordination at the hands of Bishop Hall of Exeter, one of the English delegates to the Synod of Dort, and presentation to a benefice in England; later he was a member of the Westminster Assembly and took the Solemn League and Covenant; and again with the triumph of Independency he took the Engagement also" (p. 134).

16. On the Cassel colloquy, today relegated to an unjust oblivion, cf. in addition to the article of Carl Mirbt in *Realencyklopädie für protestantische Theologie und Kirche*, 3rd ed., vol. 3, Leipzig, 1897, pp. 744-745, short treatise of Ernst Ludwig Theodor Henke, *Das Unionscolloquium zu Cassel im Juli 1661*, Marburg, 1861.

17. On the destiny of this University, founded in 1620 by the Count Ernest III of Holstein-Schaumburg and dissolved in 1809, cf. F.C. Th. Piderit, *Geschichte der Hessisch-Schaumburgischen Universität Rinteln*, without indication of place, 1842.

18. Born in 1620, Curtius (latinized form of Kurtz) did his doctorate in theology in Basel (1645), after having studied in several German universities. Rector of the Latin School of Cassel from 1647 to 1653, he was then second, then first professor of theology at the University of Marburg until his death, in 1684. - Cf. *Allgemeine deutsche Biographie*, vol. 4, Leipzig, 1876, p. 652, and Franz Gundlach, *Catalogus professorum academiae Marburgensis*, Marburg, 1927, p. 22.

19. Born in 1610, Hein (or. Heinius) from 1642 taught philosophy and pedagogy at the Herborn Gymnasium. In possession of the doctorate in theology from the University of Basel beginning in 1650, he taught the "sacred sciences" at Herborn, then from 1661, at Marburg, where he remained until his death (1686).- Cf. Freidrich Wilhelm Strieder, *Grundlage zu einer hessischen Gelehrten und Schriftsteller Geschichte seit der Reformation bis auf gegenwärtige Zeiten*, vol. 5, Cassel, 1785, pp. 376-396, and Franz Gundlach, *Catalogus professorum academiae Marburgensis*, Marburg, 1927, pp. 22-23.

20. Born in 1620, Musaeus studied at the Universities of Iena and Helmstedt where he was a student of Calixtus. Called to Rinteln in 1648 as professor of philosophy, he was there called upon to teach theology several years later. Named professor at Helmstedt in 1663, he left that city in 1665 to move to Kiel, where, in spite of illness, he pursued his professoral activity until his death in 1674. - Cf. Carl Anton Dolle, *Ausführliche lebensbeschreibung aller Professorum Theologiae, welche auf der Universität zu Rinteln vom Anfange derselben bis auf gegenwärtige Zeit gelebet und gelehret haben,* 1st part, Bückeburg, 1751, pp. 275-296, and the summaries that are given by the *Allgemeine deutsche Biographie,* vol. 23, Leipzig, 1886, pp. 90-91, and the *Realencyklopädie für protestantische Theologie und Kirche,* 3rd ed., vol. 13, Leipzig, 1903, pp. 576-577.

21. Born in 1616, Henichius (latinized form of Heneke) did his study at the University of Helmstedt where he was won over to the "unionist" ideas of Calixtus. Professor of metaphysics and Hebrew at Rinteln from 1643, he taught theology in that city for twenty years, from 1651 until his death (1671). - Cf. Carl Anton Dolle, *op. cit.,* vol. 5, pp. 441-451, and the article in the *Allgemeine deutsche Biographie,* vol. 11, Leipzig, 1880, pp. 749-750.

22. Here are the four articles to which the theologians of Marburg and Rinteln adhered:
    1. "We are all born sinners and children of wrath; but baptism is the sacrament of our regeneration, by which children are incorporated into Jesus Christ. This sacrament is necessary, a preceptual necessity, but not an absolute necessity, as if God had no other means for regenerating sinners; this is why children who die without baptism are not damned when it is not their fault, for it is not the privation, but the contempt of baptism that damns."
    2. "Jesus Christ is true God and true man in unity of person, and these two natures were united by a hypostatic union, indissoluable and with no admixture. The human nature of Jesus Christ subsists in the hypostasis of the divine nature, and then of this infinite and perfect union. All fullness of divinity lives bodily within him, and omnipotence was given to him in heaven and on earth."
    3. "God, in a movement of divine mercy, sent his son to save all men; for he was made the propitiation for our sins, and not only for ours, but for those of the whole world; and if several are damned, it is their own fault, and because of the contempt that they have had for the grace that God gave to us in Jesus Christ."
    4. "I believe that I receive in the Eucharist the true body and the true blood of Jesus Christ, with the bread and the wine, according to his saying: Take, eat, this is my body; drink, this is my blood. As to the manner in which we eat this body, I believe that it is sacramental, mystical, spiritual and that it surpasses our senses. Faith is absolutely necessary for receiving in a salvatory manner this sacrament, and those who partake of it without faith become guilty of the body and the blood of Jesus Christ."
    These four articles, as well as the deliberations of the Cassel of colloquy, are found in their original text in a *Brevis relatio colloquii authoritate... Wilhelmi Hassiae Landgravii... inter theologos quosdam Marpurgenses et Rintelenses, celsitudinis suae mandato convocatos, Cassellis die 1. iulii et aliquot seqq-habiti,* published in Cassel in 1661 and translated into German, the same year, under the title *Kurtzer Bericht von dem colloquio...*

23. In 1662, they opened fire on the participants of the Cassel Colloquy by the publication of a treatise entitled *Epicrisis de colloquio Cassellano Rinthelio-Marpurgensium* to which the Rinteln theologians, affirming their fidelity to the Augsburg Confession, responded in the *Ad invariatae Augustanae confessioni addictas academias et ministeria epistola apologetica facultatis theologicae in academia Rinthelensi.*

24. The dedicatory epistle of the Εἰρηνικὸν opens with the reminder of the 1631 ordinance ("Cum Synodus Carentonensis, anno M. DC. XXXI, viam ad concordiam inter Evangelicos constituendam, sapienter et Christiane munivisset, dici non potest . . . p. I).

25. Cf. Εἰρηνικόν, p. V and pp. VII-VIII.

26. Cf. Carl Wilhelm Hering, *Geschichte der kirchlichen Unionsversuche seit der Reformation bis auf unsere Zeit,* vol. 2, Leipzig 1838, p. 135. The problem of Protestant reconciliation could not escape being posed to the admiral's descendant sincerely Reformed, in George II of Würtemberg, she had married a convinced Lutheran (cf. Max Geiger, *Die Basler Kirche und Theologie im Zeitalter der Hochorthodoxie,* Zollikon-Zürich, 1952, p. 86).

27. The title he gave to it was not new. François du Jon of Berry, called Franciscus Junius (1545-1602), had already composed an *Eirenicum* in: *Opera theologica,* col. 677-762, Geneva, 1607). David Pareus (1548-1622), professor at Heidelberg, student of Ursinus and teacher of Comenius, had published in turn, in 1614, an *Irenicum* which exercised a considerable influence and of which Amyraut was seemingly aware (cf. *De secessione,* p. 164, and Εἰρηνικόν, p. 359, where the *Irenicum* mentioned is doubtless that of Pareus). Finally, Daniel Zwicker (1612-1678), of Dantzig, had anonymously published, in 1658, an *Irenicum Irenicorum* (cf. *A History of the Ecumenical Movement,* p. 757, pp. 86-87 and p. 78).

28. Rare as well, this work was printed on the press of Isaac Desbordes. In *Die Protestantischen Centraldogmen in ihrer Entwicklung innerhalb der reformierten Kirche* (cf. vol. 2, Zurich, 1856, p. 506), Alexander Schweizer mentions, in addition to the Saumur edition, an edition published in Hanau (Hesse-Nassau), in 1664, whose existence we were unable to verify. The Εἰρηνικόν will be designated in the text of this lecture by the number: 2.

29. Cf. Charles-Edmond Saigey, *Moïse Amyraut: sa vie et ses écrits,* Strasbourg, 1849, p. 33.

30. To the problem of baptism, Amyraut dedicates chapter 4 of the *De secessione* (pp. 63-78) and chapter 9 of the Εἰρηνικόν (p. 195-220).

31. In the *De secessione,* Amyraut dedicates but four pages (pp. 74-78) to the question of baptism as such. Thus, he takes no time for any of the problems brought out in the Εἰρηνικόν; exorcism itself provokes there no commentary.

32. Born in 1582, Gerhard was professor at the University of Iena, from 1616 to his death (1637). His *Loci Theologici,* published from 1610 to 1622, earned for him, and rightly so, the reputation as the most significant representative of Lutheran orthodoxy.

33. Cf. *Brevis relatio colloquii . . . inter theologos quosdam Marpurgenses et Rintelenses . . .,* pp. 17 sq.

34. Amyraut dedicates chapter 5 of the *De secessione* (pp. 79-127) and chapter 10 of the Εἰρηνικόν (pp. 220-279) to the examination of the Lord's Supper.

35. The sole passage of the Εἰρηνικόν which signifies any progress with respect to the *De secessione* is that which Amyraut dedicates to a methodical confrontation of the eucharistic doctrine of the *Regula credendi et vivendi ad reginam christinam transmissa* (Lutheran writing whose author has remained anonymous) with that of the Reformed churches (cf. Εἰρηνικόν, pp. 258-269). In its greater part, chapter 10 of the Εἰρηνικόν consists of a detailed presentation from the Reformed point of view (pp. 222-258), during which the Saumur theologian completely forgets his Lutheran interlocutors.

36. Cf. Εἰρηνικόν, p. 370. - Contrary to that which the Saumur theologian believed, Luther taught the doctrine of ubiquity in the sermon *Vom Sakrament des Leibes* (1526), in the treatise directed against Zwingli and Oecolampadius, *Dass diese Worte, das ist mein Leib, noch Feststehen* (1527), and in the declaration of faith Vom Abendmahl Christi (1528), in particular.

37. Cf. Article X: "Von dem Abendmahl des Herren wird also gelehrt, dass wahrer Leib und Blut Christi wahrhaftiglich unter der Gestalt des Brots und Weins im Abendmahl gegenwärtig sei und da ausgeteilt und genommen werde. Derhalben wird auch die Gegenlehr verworfen" (*Die Bekenntnisschriften der evangelisch-lutherischen Kirche,* Göttingen, 4th ed., 1959, p. 64).

38. "Quum igitur neque cultus apud Lutheranos per se conscientiam polluat, neque declaratio fidei quenquam ad dogmatis istius de ubiquitate susceptionem aut professionem adstringat, non video cur eorum communio, quorum pietatem ex utraque illa re metiri nos oportet, nobis sit repudianda" *(De secessione,* pp. 104).

39. "Ratio igitur pacificandae istius controversiae in eo videtur esse posita, ut communi quadam fidei declaratione explicetur quod utrinque in confesso est; nimirum corpus Christi esse in Eucharistia realiter et sacramentaliter tamen. Interpretatio vero utrique parti permittenda esset ea lege atque conditione ut utrinque et in concionibus publicis, et in privatis sermonibus, et in scriptis operibus quae de religione componuntur, diligenter abstineatur ab omnibus contentionibus omnibusque verbis acrioribus ac immoderatioribus, quae vulnus aliquod fraternae concordiae infligere queant" (*De secessione,* pp. 117-118).

40. To Christology, Amyraut dedicates the 6th chapter of the *De secessione* (pp. 127-156) and the 11th chapter of the Ειρηνικον (pp. 280-298).

41. Cf. the adverb ασυγχυτος (inconfuse) of the Chalcedon definition.

42. Cf. the adverb ατρεπτος (immutabiliter) of the Chalcedon definition

43. Cf. the adverb αδιακριτος (indivise) and αχωριστος (inseparabiliter) of the Chalcedon definition.

44. Amyraut dedicates to the study of predestination Chapter 7 of the *De secessione* (pp. 156-191) and Chapter 12 of the Ειρηνικον, pp. 298-313).

45. Cf. Jean Aymon, *Actes ecclésiastiques et civils de tous les Synodes nationaux des Églises réformées de France,* La Haye, vol. 2, 1710, pp. 182-184.

46. Cf. Jean Aymon, *op. cit.,* vol. 2, p. 311.

47. "Following the indulgence that one had for the Lutherans, John Cameron, Scotsman, celebrated minister and theology professor in the Academy of Saumur, there taught a call and a universal grace, which declared itself to all men through the wonders of the works of God, by His Word and the sacraments. This doctrine of Cameron's was strongly and ingeniously defended by Amyraut and Testard his disciples, theology professors in the same city. This entire Academy embraced it..." (Bossuet, *op. cit.,* vol. 3, Paris, 1770, p. 105).

48. François Laplanche himself feels that the opinion of Bossuet is "certainly exaggerated" (cf. *Orthodoxie et prédication. L'oeuvre d'Amyraut et la querelle de la grâce universelle,* p. 272).

49. Our statement would be incomplete if we did not bring out the fact that, in the *De secessione,* the chapter on predestination closes with an exposition (pp. 187-191) designed to show that with regard to the Arminians, the Lutherans are in agreement with the Reformed.

50. To the question of Providence, Amyraut dedicates chapter 8 of *De secessione* (pp. 191-206) and the chapter 13 of the Ειρηνικον (pp. 313-340).

51. Alexander Schweizer facilitates the task considerably when, in order to explain the Amyraldian conception of Providence, he only quotes those texts where the Saumur theologian limits himself to speaking of the manner in which this providence allows evil to act (cf. *Die protestantischen Centraldogmen in ihrer Entwicklung innerhalb der reformierten Kirche,* Zürich, vol. 2, 1856, pp. 514-516).

52. Amyraut examines the means to reach unity in chapter 12 of the *De secessione* (pp. 263-283), - after having already taken them up in certain passages of chapters 9 (pp. 236-242 and p. 245) and 10 (pp. 253-255 and pp. 262-263) of the same work - and, especially, in chapter 14 of the Ειρηνικον (pp. 341-403).

53. The *De secessione* is very brief on the "ecumenical" role of the synods (pp. 250-255). On the other hand, it implies how painful it was for the French Reformed to be unable to participate, because of royal prohibitions, in international Protestant encounters such as the Synod of Dort (cf. p. 251).

54. To the duty of princes, Amyraut dedicates but one page in the *De secessione* (p. 265). The discussion of the same problem occupies eight pages in the Ειρηνικόν. That indicates that doubtless because of the growing hostility of French royalty to the Reformed, Amyraut turned always more to the side of the German Protestant princes, the only ones capable in his eyes of reconciling the churches born of the reformation (cf. Ειρηνικόν, p. 402).

55. All during this lecture, we have called the members of the Reformed churches and those of the Augsburg Confession by the name of the Reformers whose name they claim. We must remark, however, that for Amyraut, the terms "Calvinists" and "Lutherans," without being reprehensible, should be nonetheless banished, "because we have only one Teacher and only one Master, Jesus Christ, our Lord" (2, p. 5).

56. We are thinking in particular of the determinative role that, according to the conceptions of the period, Amyraut attributes to the secular power.

57. Cf. in particular this characteristic passage from the Ειρηνικόν: "Quae est universi generis humani in varias societates distributio, ea fere est Ecclesiae Christianae dispertitio in varias communiones. Ut igitur rerumpublicarum formae adeo diversae sunt inter ipsas, ut vix duas reperias quae sibi invicem repondeant ad amussim: sic vix est ut duas Christianorum communiones observare possimus, inter quas non aliquod magnum et memorabile discrimen intercedat. Tantum, istud videndum est, num quemadmodum omnes respublicae inter se pacem et amicitiam colere possunt, nisi siqua sit quam bar-baries efferaverit, et extra communes humanitatis oras extulerit, sic etiam omnes Christianorum communiones inter se concordiam alere licitum sit" (p. 350).

58. It is thus that the desire for truth obliges Amyraut to exclude, apart from the Roman Church, Anabaptists, Socinians and Arminians whose doctrine appears to him to cheapen certain essential areas of the faith (cf. Ειρηνικόν, pp. 4-5).

59. The Quaker authors all admit that the Saumur theologian exercised a decisive influence on William Penn. Thus Bonamy Dobree writes: "Amyraut was clearly one of the major influences in the formation of Penn's mind... Like the Quakers, Amyraut believed that Christianity and war were impossible bedfellows. Above all, he was of a large and tolerant temper, working hard and successfully (!) for the union of the Protestant churches in France; there was no narrow sectarianism about him" (*William Penn: Quaker and Pioneer*, London, 1932, p. 19 and p. 20). See also Mabel Richmond Brailsford, *The Making of William Penn*, London and New York, 1930, pp. 111-124.

60. In addition to the influence of Amyraut, that of John Dury, the great Scotch "unionist," was exercised on William Penn. Cf. *A History of the Ecumenical Movement*. London, 1954, p. 98.

D'Huisseau, Advocate of Reconciliation Between All Christian Confessions

In his work on *Louis XIV et les protestants* [1], Jean Orcibal described in excellent terms the relations which existed between Catholics and Protestants at the beginning of the personal reign of the Sun King. In spite of the repressive measures which had begun to fall upon the Reformed and which, in their eyes, already constituted a "persecution;" the reconciliation of the churches was a subject of preoccupation for each of the religious parties. On both sides, theologians attempted to discover the proper means for bringing an end to the schism that was tearing Christendom apart. This reconciliation movement was to be accentuated even more thanks to the conversion of Marshal Turenne, in October of 1668. Won over to Catholicism, the Marshal used the leisure time left to him by the peace of Aix-la-Chapelle (May 2, 1669) to attempt to reunite (finding his inspiration in the plans of Richelieu and the nuncio Bargellini) those who are today called "separated brethren." The conversations thus held between priests and ministers resulted in putting aside a number of controversies. "Not that," as Alfred Rébelliau rightly points out, "agreement on those points was reached; not that, even, it was effortless or close at hand; but that (and here was the great step made) the moderates of both parties considered it possible"[2]. This situation was favorable to the project of D'Huisseau. In a first section, I will examine the strange conditions in which this project was made known. In a second section, I shall examine his "ecumenical" thought. In a third section, lastly, I want to survey the harsh polemics that his thought produced in French reformed churches.

In 1670 at Saumur there appeared in anonymity, a work entitled *La reunion du christianisme ou la manière de rejoindre tous les chrèstiens sous une seule confession de foy* [3]. There was no lack of wondering who might be its author. Public opinion and the authorities of the Reformed Churches believed to have discovered him in the person of the pastor Isaac D'Huisseau[4]. This man was no late-comer. Sixty-three years of age, he had exercised the pastoral ministry in Saumur for approximately forty years. On three occasions, his role as pastor, making him eligible for such functions, he had been elevated to the dignity of rector of the Academy. But, in particular, he had rendered an immense service to the Reformed Churches of France by establishing, beginning in 1650, the text of their *Discipline,* flawed up until that time by numerous variants and marred with grave errors [5].

Summoned to declare whether or not he had taken part in the composition of the treatise on *La reunion du christianisme,* D'Huisseau always refused to answer either by yes or no. In the declaration that he made before the Synod of Anjou in his own defense, he affirmed that he was not responsible for the publication of this work, and that, if he had intended to edit any writing, he would have submitted it beforehand to the censorship of his brethren; that he did not feel obliged to reveal what he might know concerning "the author who would have put his thoughts on paper with no ill intentions"[6].

Why such an attitude? Must one really accept the explanation of Lefèvre, one of the professors of the Saumur academy implicated in this affair, in which anonymity surrounding the author of the book of *La réunion* had no other goal but to encourage an enterprise which, in order to have some chance of success, had to appear as being advocated by "a completely disinterested person"[7]? This is not an unlikely explanation. It is difficult to understand, however, that, summoned to explain himself and deliver the key to the mystery, D'Huisseau remained silent. Must one attribute his obstinate silence to the fear of ecclesiastical punishment? We give little consideration to this opinion since his refusal to deliver the solution to the riddle cost him the heaviest of punishments. One must suppose that the strange behavior of D'Huisseau is due to the fact that, as Richard Simon claims, *La réunion du christianisme* was more the manifesto of a theological faction than the "work of an individual"[8]? This hypothesis is tempting, and seems to find some support in the proceedings of the Anjou Synod of 1670[9]. These proceedings reveal that three professors of the Saumur Academy were, to varying degrees, involved in the secret of the work. These include the Hellenist Tanneguy Lefèvre [10], one of the most remarkable scholars of his time, the Hebraist Jacques Cappel [11], whose father was one of the founders of biblical criticism, and the philosopher Pierre de Villemandy[12], successor of the Genevan Chouet who introduced Cartesianism at Saumur. If the participation of Cappel and that of Villemandy must be excluded, the role of Lefèvre, on the other hand, was predominant according to the proceedings of the synod: it was he in person who, while D'Huisseau was absent from Saumur, gave the printer the manuscript of *La ré-union du christianisme* which he apparently received from Paris from an unknown sender; it was he who corrected its drafts; it was he, final-ly, who composed the commendation of the concord in Latin verse which was inscribed above the work. These indications are certainly not negligible. They do not, however, enable us to discover the author of the book *La réunion.*

The solution to the riddle is furnished by a letter that the son of D'Huisseau, who had taken refuge in London, addressed to Elie Benoist, August 27, 1695, asking him to correct in the *Histoire de l'édit de Nantes* the passages referring to his deceased father[13]. Pro-foundly rankled by the manner in which his father is treated by Benoist, the younger D'Huisseau insists upon re-establishing the truth. After having brought out the fact that his father never had the least intention to favor the purposes of the Romanist religion, he underlines the fact that *Le réunion du christianisme* had "but one sole author and, until the time of its publication, one sole partisan and approver" (fo 23). This author is none other than the editor of the *Discipline des Églises réformées de France.* "Scandalized" by the num-erous divisions of Christianity, "believing that it was of the charity of all Christians to remedy this disorder," D'Huisseau "threw himself little by little into the feelings of a tolerance that might appear a bit exaggerated" (fo 23). And when divers propositions of reunion were made, according to the views of the Court of France, he believed that the view that he had in mind, which was sincere and which he esteemed only the legitimate one, would dissipate all false and wrong ideas, as the light of the sun darkens and dissipates that of terrestrial lights" (fo 23). It is thus that D'Huisseau composed *La réunion du christianisme* toward the end of the year 1669 (cf. fo 23 vo).

The circumstances of the composition of our work having been thus elucidated, what were those of its publication? According to the younger D'Huisseau, his father circulated the manuscript that he had produced to "certain persons among his friends" (fo 23 vo). Du Soul [14], Villemandy, Cappel, Pajon[15], Lefèvre et Crespin [16] saw the text that later was to be incriminated. The first four among them weakly approved it, but the last two, "minds little illuminated in mat-ters of theology and capable of somewhat visionary hopes" (fo 23 vo), praised it beyond all measure, imagining that it was to re-establish peace between Christians. Taking advantage of D'Huisseau's absence, Lefevre, in his enthusiasm, gave the manuscript of the book *La réunion* into the hands of the publisher Rene Péan, without submitting it to the provincial censors and without showing it to Claude[17], as the author would have wished. (cf. fo 23 vo).

The explanations of the younger D'Huisseau are convincing. One important point, however, remains obscure. Why did the elder D'Huisseau refuse to admit that he was the author of *La réunion du christianisme?* The letter to Elie Benoist does not elude this question, but gives the following answer. The book *La réunion* having been "condemned for socinianism and for divers other things which are in no wise tolerated in France" (fo 24 vo), certain Protestants intended to pursue the author in court. To denounce oneself in such conditions"... would be an act of inhumanity" (fo 24 vo). Indeed, such is the thinking of the young D'Huisseau: the authorities would have been able to take advantage of his father's avowal; by threatening him with judiciary prosecution, they would have been able to force him to abjure.

Whatever one might think of the motives attributed to his father's silence by the younger D'Huisseau, the indications that the latter gives in his letter to Elie Benoist solve, it seems to us, the majority of the riddles that until now have surrounded the origin of *La réunion du christianisme.* D'Huisseau is responsible for its composition: Lefevre, for its distribution. The conjoint action of these two men, otherwise quite different from one another, was to provoke profound emotion within French Protestantism. In order to understand the reasons for this, it is necessary to examine the contents of *La réunion.*

II

The preface of *La réunion* reveals to the reader at the outset the designs pursued by its author. Saddened to "see the holy religion that the Son of God brought from heaven to earth, miserably torn by so many divers sects" (p. 1), indignant in observing that "there has not been found, up until now, any person who would have attempted, with any success, to cure such a great illness" (pp. 1-11), D'Huisseau avows having given himself over, for several years, to a "serious meditation" on remedying these divisions. He holds that he has discovered "the sole means for reconciling all those who make a profession of Christianity" (p. VII). Because he distrusted his own strength (cf. p. IX) and knew the imperfections of his style (cf. p. XI) he hesitated at length before delivering to the public the fruit of his reflections. He made his decision, finally, in the hope that one of "these fine geniuses of the age" would finish his outline (p. XI). As he began to work, he attempted to make himself intelligible to all and to remove himself from all prejudice . "I avoided as a dangerous snag," he writes, "to give the least suspicion that I have an interest in any of the parties" (p. XV). This difficult undertaking which prompted him to remain anonymous, was thoroughly accomplished in his work.

In the first part of *La reunion du christianisme,* D'Huisseau examines the nature and the consequences of the division. He deplores the quarrels that tear Christianity apart . "Is it not something very sad and an unfortunate example," he sighs, "to see Christians as miserably divided as they are today!" (pp. 8-9). "There is no truly Christian soul that does not cry out in seeing the effects of the aversions and implacable hatred that exist between those it recognizes as its brothers" (pp. 9-10) While he is sensitive to the divisions that separate Protestants and Catholics, the author does not intend to limit his plan of reunion to them alone. "I have the design," he writes, "to reunite the Christians of the Orient with those of the Occident, the Greeks and the Romans, the Catholics and the Protestants, and all the diverse branches into which the latter have divided themselves"(p. 13). Division is indeed odious, not only because it disfigures "the face of Christianity" (p. 14), but also because in compromising charity, it threatens sanctification, because it develops ungodliness, irreligion, atheism [18]; because it hinders the work of missions; because it dismembers the church - none of the existing "Christian societies" constitute the body of Christ (p. 48), the Church is "like the pitiful wreck of a vessel that has lost its way" (p. 53); because it produces innumerable wars; because, finally, it aids the advance of the Turks.

Having thus enumerated the pernicious effects of division, D'Huisseau seeks in his second section to detect its causes. The vanity and the pride of men contribute much to it. Instead of conserving "Christian doctrine such as ... was given by the Son of God and proposed by his apostles" (p. 60), its purity and holiness had been altered. Its original simplicity had been lost by overloading it with foreign elements .The book *La reunion* takes up here a distinction established by Calvin, a distinction utilized by Philippe du Plessis-Mornay, founder of the Saumur Academy[19]., and, in the 17th century, by the Arminian Hugo Grotius as well as by the Lutheran George Calixtus. D'Huisseau holds that, indeed, "there are in religion essential and fundamental doctrines from which one cannot depart without giving notable prejudice to religion and to the salvation of souls" and "there are others... which are of lesser importance... where one can hold such or such an opinion without injuring one's conscience" (p. 69).

If division among Christians originates from failing to recall this distinction, it has, for D'Huisseau, yet other causes. This division is also due to the fact that one has deviated from Holy Scripture, in attributing to men as much authority and infallibility as to God. It flows as well from having forsaken the simplicity of primitive Christianity, which included but very few doctrines, in favor of the forging of "dogmas" and "abstruse mysteries" (p. 88). Instead of holding to the Apostle's Creed which encloses the essentials, "the schools of Plato and Aristotle" have been consulted in the area of dogmatics (p. 90). Finally, there has been a last cause of division: religion has become a "specious pretext" permitting certain ones to "advance their affairs" and to "establish their fortune in the world" (p. 93).

In the third part of his work far and away the most interesting, D'Huisseau exposes "the proper means for reuniting all Christians into a single communion" (p. 101). Before delivering his own solution, he is intent upon showing why all the efforts attempted before him were condemned to failure. "They have always built upon this poor foundation," he writes, "that the evil was in and of itself incurable, and that consequently it was enough to study how to stop the course of its most inconvenient symptoms. They thought that it was only a question of lengthening the languishing life of the sick one, whose recovery was, is it were, deplored. They had not thought of the means of reuniting all the societies of Christians into one. They believed that the difference in their feelings was too great, and in matters too important, to make them agree upon all the terms that could bring them to agreement" (p. 102-103). Deploring the fact that a general agreement was not sought after, our author brings out that, in order to favor the reunion of limited societies, "a certain mixture of doctrines had been made and a composition of things that can never be amalgamated, instead of working to purify Christian doctrines, to set them apart from the mixture of all foreign things and to bring them back to their first simplicity" (p. 107).

After this criticism, which seems to reveal either a certain naïvety or a certain presumption, D'Huisseau presents the five aspects of the proposal that he has devised. It is necessary, first of all, to "strip oneself of all bias and to disengage oneself from all personal interests in order to propose but the glory of God and the salvation of souls" (p. 110). But how might one achieve this? Our author proposes a method finding its inspiration in Descartes, whose thought had been accepted in Saumur since the teaching of the Genevan Chouet [20]. "There has been proposed for some time now in philosophy," he writes, "a means of reasoning well and of taking sure steps toward truth. It is held that for this one must detach oneself from all preconceived opinions and from all mental prejudices, that one must first entertain only the simplest notions and the propositions which can not be contested by anyone with the faintest ability to reason. Can we not imitate this method in religion? Can we not put aside for a time all those opinions that we heretofore defended with such warmth, in order to examine them afterwards with freedom and without any passion, holding to our common principle which is Holy Scripture? Would it not be possible that we consider without any commitment the foundation of religion generally recognized by all who profess to be Christians, and the maxims on which all are agreed? Would it not be an infallible means for recognizing, with a disinterested mind, how we must advance along an unknown path, and how we might build upon a foundation that is solid and approved by each one?" (pp. 117-119).

In recommending this method, D'Huisseau denies having wished to "establish indifference and leave minds unsettled" (p. 122). He shows this when, proposing his second means for arriving at unity, he holds that Christians must rely upon a foundation "which is firm and solid, and upon which everybody agrees" (p. 122). This foundation is first of all Scripture, and then, the Apostle's Creed considered as "an extract and a short form of the gospel" (p. 124). Faithful to the scriptural principle, unconscious as well of the fact that the Bible does not furnish an elaborated theology in all its details, our author considers with suspicion all doctrines presented as "explanations, elucidations and consequences" taken from Scripture (p. 126). Such doctrines are but "efforts of the human mind" (p. 126). In the same way as the confessions of faith particular to each Christian society, they are subject to error; they constitute at the same time possible causes of division.

Having thus affirmed the authority of the Bible, D'Huisseau

distinguishes in Scripture - we now come to his third means for reuniting Christians - three kinds of teaching: dogmas first of all, then disciplinary and liturgical rules, and finally moral precepts. The latter, which constitute "one of the principal articles of religion" and even "the most important" (p. 133), should not incite any dispute: the Law and the summary that Christ took from it are recognized by all Christians. In the area of ecclastiastical discipline, Scripture does not prescribe for us "point by point and in detail all that must take place" (p. 133); it rather contents itself with giving us "a few general precepts" (p. 134). Provided that they show themselves respectful of order and decency, provided as well that they conserve the fundamental points of religion, Christians have at their disposition here a freedom which will take into account "places, times and persons" (p. 134). It would, therefore be, "unreasonable... to cause schism in the church concerning the order which should exist between her leaders," unreasonable to break the union "because some desire that the church be directed by bishops, and others that there be equality among the pastors" (p. 135-136). Disposing thus of questions of ecclessiastical organization, D'Huisseau shows that liturgical traditions do not justify the division of Christianity. It is not admissible over "some diversity of vestments of those who officiate in the Church, that the knot be broken that should hold all Christians together." It is not right that over "the ornaments of the church buildings, the attitude which individuals must hold in acts of devotion, and other such ceremonies, one ruin the peace of the church and the relations among her members" (p. 136). On the whole, since neither moral precepts nor disciplinary and liturgical rules are of such a nature as to divide Christians, "there should be no occasion of dispute other than regarding the dogmas which are proposed to the faith" (p. 131).

The book *La réunion* does not limit itself to reducing thus the causes of separation. Even within those truths that "the faithful must receive by faith" (p. 143), D'Huisseau produces - this is his fourth means to overcome the schism - a new line of reasoning. He distinguishes indeed in Scripture between "mysteries of religion," "historical narrations," and "predictions" (prophecies, as we would say today) (p. 144). The historical narrations "must not and cannot give any room for contention and even less for division" (p. 144). The problems of chronology and interpretation that they pose, provided that the fundamental doctrines be recognized, must be placed before the free judgement of each one. This is the case as well for the predictions. "They too must not be the subject of any division" (p. 146). If one believes in their future fulfillment, one can then inquire freely as to their meaning and to the moment of their realization.

After having eliminated thus the historical narrations and the predictions, D'Huisseau retains only the mysteries of religion as eventual causes of division. In this area, however, he once again narrows the area of conflict: this is his fifth means for preventing discord among Christians! Utilizing the distinction of Calvin, he discerns in religion "important dogmas, essential, fundamental and necessary to salvation," and "other less important ones, that one can ignore, and where even some error might slip in, without either salvation, the peace of consciences or the tranquillity of the church being compromised" (p. 150). But where is one to find the criterion for this distinction? To this question, our author responds that, since Scripture does not address itself to this question "in formal terms," it is necessary to consider as fundamental "all that which is clearly proposed in the Word of God and which is also received by general avowal" (p. 152). The doctrines which are not revealed with clarity in the Bible, but which have been elaborated by theologians working from scriptural data, can in no way be essential [21]. Liable to being interpreted in different ways, they can indeed "show signs of the weaknesses and the imperfection of the human mind" (p. 154).

But which are for D'Huisseau the essential doctrines? Having already brought out that they are those of the Apostle's Creed, he now shows the content of this declaration of faith. He retains thus the oneness of God, the redemptive mission, the death, the resurrection and the return of Christ as judge of the living and the dead, as well as "such other truths that Christians admit as being very distinctly taught in Holy Scripture" (p. 155). Explicitly excluded from the catalog of the fundamental points are the "doctrines which establish the order of God's eternal decrees, which say precisely which is the object of predestination, which expose how the two natures are united in the person of Jesus Christ, which delve into the mystery of the Trinity, which affirm having discovered the means by which the Holy Spirit acts in the hearts of the faithful, and other things of a similar nature" (p. 155).

To illustrate his position and prove that "one can work out one's own salvation in Christianity without throwing oneself into the confusion of all these prickly questions of the schools" (p. 160), D'Huisseau imagines the case of a Christian who would know but the rudiments of the Creed and who would be "carried by the tempest into the Magellana [22] or into some other country whose inhabitants would never have heard of our mysteries" (p. 160). "I pose the case," writes our author, "that he be only persuaded of these truths: that there be a God who created heaven and earth; that he asks of us an accomplished holiness; that we have transgressed his ordinances, which renders us unfit for his grace; that, however he invites us to repentance and to salvation; that he has sent for this effect the one that he himself calls his Son; that this Son died for our sins; that he rose from the dead for our justification; that he ascended into heaven, and that he there intercedes for us: and that, provided that we be fully persuaded of these truths, and that we apply ourselves to godliness toward God and to charity toward our neighbor, we will obtain eternal happiness. I suppose finally that this man teaches these things to these savage nations, and that these peoples who had until then ignored all these truths, be touched by their beauty, and then that they be fully persuaded of them and that they conform their lives to them. I ask if these people cannot be said to be truly Christian and if they are not on the path of salvation. As for me, I have no difficulty with this, and going even further, I would say that I would hold them far happier if they abide in these principles, than if one came to overload them with all these curious questions which are ordinarily maintained." (p. 161-162).

This section whose generosity does not succeed in veiling its doctrinal indifference, completes, in our work, the theological study as such. After having presented the five means for "reuniting all Christians into the same denomination" (p. 164), D'Huisseau examines the proper "paths" to make easier the execution of his plan (p. 164). Desirous of proving that his views are in no wise illusory, he holds that it is necessary to encourage the diffusion of a "unionist" literature, to favor interconfessional conversations [23], and to stimulate the princes who can "strike the sharpest blows at this occasion"[24] (p. 173).

But D'Huisseau does not content himself with this position. He refutes in advance a certain number of objections. To those who will blame him for being opposed in his plan to inevitable divisions, as inevitable as "the course of the stars" and "revolving of the seasons"

(p. 177), he announces his hope for a "general peace among all Christians" (p. 179-180). To those who will accuse him of deviating from the apostle's doctrine by reducing the Christian faith to a few fundamental points, he answers (but does he truly refute the accusation?) that if the apostles were intransigent with heresiarchs, that they were patient and gentle with the victims of heresy. To those who will suspect him of having favored "indifference" and the "despising of all religion" - this suspicion appears "atrocious" to him (p. 183) - he affirms that he has limited himself, by discharging from religion "curious and strange questions" (p. 185), "to return to the simplest and most naive doctrine of the gospel" (p. 184). To those, finally, who affirm that his plan is unachievable, he declares his conviction that, "provided that one desire to carry it forth with zeal and for religious motives, this affair will be able to succeed for the great good of all Christendom" (p. 187). With an optimism which does not correspond to historical reality, he sees in the Marburg conference (1529) and in the Poissy Colloquy (1561) (which, according to him, came very close to succeeding) examples showing that reconciliation is possible. He, therefore, invites Christians to manifest "a fraternal and charitable tolerance" (p. 189) and to agree upon the fundamental points capable of uniting them (cf. p. 192).

In conclusion, D'Huisseau summarizes the advantages that his plan offers. By abolishing all division within Christendom, the graces which were enjoyed by the first believers will be recovered, "one will find much greater facility for extirpating vice and working toward the reformation of morals in society" (p. 196); the States will be assured of a political stability which will permit them to unite themselves against the Turks; the clergymen will be delivered from the worry of knowing whether or not they are following the right direction in their teaching [25]; "several peoples which now look upon it with only aversion or contempt" (p. 204) will be attracted to the Gospel; finally, the celestial spirits and God himself will be filled with joy.

As our analysis shows, *La réunion du christianisme* testifies to a singular audacity in the area of doctrine. Concerned above all with high-lighting the moral teaching of Christianity (cf. p. 133) - by this feature he prefigures the attitude of 19th century Protestantism -- D'Huisseau cheerfully sacrifices ecclesiology to the cause of unity (cf. p. 136). As Joseph Prost has remarked, he is disposed to "make *tabula rasa* of the whole visible church"[26]. In dodging with somewhat surprising ease questions of ecclesiastical structure and organization [27], the editor of the *Discipline des Églises réformées de France* simply pushes to their extreme the principles exposed by du Plessis-Mornay in his *Traité de l'Église* (1578) and utilized by the school of Arminius.

But D'Huisseau does not limit himself to eliminating ecclesiology. He manifests a veritable phobia with respect to that which he calls "curious and strange questions" (pp. 162 and 185), "curious and useless questions" (p. 202) and the "prickly questions of the schools" (p. 160). What he is here aiming at he shows clearly when he formulates the embryonic Creed that he is disposed to retain.[28] Utilizing in its most restrictive sense the distinction between secondary points and fundamental points [29], he first takes aim at Reformed orthodoxy. He categorically rejects the dogma of double predestination such as it had been defined, following Theodore Beza [30], by Calvin's heirs. He thus turns back- the fact is undeniable- to the position of Arminius who had been condemned by the Synod of Dort (1619) and who, reproved in turn by the Synod of Alès (1620), had succeeded nonetheless in winning in France a certain number of partisans [31].

D'Huisseau, however, does not content himself with adopting the ideas of Arminius. Rejecting Reformed orthodoxy, he shows himself to be heterodox as well when he treats the fundamentals of the Christian faith. Hiding in no way his distrust for the dogma of the Trinity and that of the two natures of Christ (cf. p. 155), he excludes them from the fundamental points. Even more, he shows himself ready to relegate them to oblivion, for he suspects them of being but the "personal opinion" of some doctor (cf. p. 156). Thus D'Huisseau is not far from Socinus who called in question the existence of three persons in God and rejected the essential divinity of Christ. By this theological radicalism, he furnished ammunition, as we shall see, for those who, in Saumur or elsewhere, seem to have vowed a solid enmity toward him.

III

The publication of *La réunion du christianisme* was favorably received at Saumur. It aroused such an approval that Richard Simon was able to say [32], echoing one of D'Huisseau's partisans, that the entire Academy was interested in it. But the situation evolved rapidly. The work published under the cloak of anonymity did not delay, indeed, in troubling the Reformed circles of the Anjou province. Its doctrinal latitudinarianism and its untimeliness offered them cause for worry. But this was not, as Elie Benoist thought [33], the only cause of its unpopularity. The book *La réunion* produced a scandal by reason of the identity of its author. D'Huisseau counted a number of adversaries among his co-religionists in Saumur. For several reasons which we cannot at this point elaborate, he had alienated himself from the good graces of the disciples of Moïse Amyraut, led by professor Etienne Gaussen[34] and Pastor Beaujardin [35].

The day that the rumor spread identifying D'Huisseau as the author of *La réunion du christianisme,* the Amyraldians realized that they held the right pretext for discrediting their opponent. They began to reproach him with being the accomplice of "superior powers," who were working in the French kingdom toward the winning over of the Protestants. They presented him as a libertine who placed "all religions into indifference"[36] and who inclined toward Socinianism. They accused him of no longer being a part of "the Religion" and of abiding therein "only in order to betray it"[37]. Denounced by three laymen, D'Huisseau was compelled to appear before the Saumur Consistory. Assisted by the Academic Council and by the king's counsel, François de Haumont [38], the Consistory deposed D'Huisseau and excommunicated him.

This excessive condemnation, contrary to the *Discipline des Églises réformées de France* aroused the indignation of D'Huisseau's partisans. They published, one after another, several works to defend their friend. Inediting, firstly, the (French) *Traduction du traité de Samuel Petit, professeur en théologie à Nîmes, touchant la réunion des chrestiens* [39], they intended to show that another Protestant theologian, whose loyalty had never been suspected, had also employed "unionist" language. And in having this translation preceeded by a *Lettre à Monsieur D'Huisseau,* they found the means to award a certificate of orthodoxy to the author of *La réunion du christianisme.* Not contenting themselves with this first publication, D'Huisseau's partisans then launched an *Apologie pour le livre intitulé la Réunion du christianisme et pour celuy qui en esté soupçonne' l'autheur à Saumur* [40]; they attempted to prove that the work censored by the Reformed authorities was neither inopportune, nor crypto-catholic, nor Pyrrhonian, nor Socinian. Finally, in a third writing, the *Examen du jugement rendu contre Monsieur D'Huisseau par les Compagnies consistoriale et academique de Saumur* [41], the friends of the condemned pastor held that the sentence carried out against him was contrary to "all the rules of ecclesiastical justice and ... to all the maxims of natural equity" (pp. 60-61).

All of these works were anonymous. Though they were the object of no retaliation - it would have been difficult to answer certain criticisms that they aimed at Gaussen - the Amyraldian party was by no means disarmed. D'Huisseau's adversaries, supported by all those who were sincerely troubled by the book *La réunion*, prepared themselves to strike a new blow in the framework of the Synod of the Anjou province, whose convocation was imminent. They acted in such fashion that, when the Synod opened in Saumur, September 18, 1670, a large majority of the representatives had already formed an unfavorable opinion concerning *La réunion du christianisme* and its author. Called upon to appear before them, D'Huisseau read a declaration in which he proclaimed his faithfulness to the Reformed faith, in which he affirmed himself ready to condemn the errors discovered in the book *La réunion*, and in which, probably referring implicitly to the role of Tanneguy Lefèvre, he maintained that he was not responsible for its publication. By obstinately refusing to avow the name of the author of the incriminated writing, he likely confirmed the members of the Synod in the paltry opinion that they held concerning him. Gaussen and Beaujardin accomplished the rest. In spite of the depositions that Cappel, Lefevre and Villemandy, professors at the Academy, made in his favor, D'Huisseau was unable to escape the judges' severity: for the second time, he was deposed and excommunicated.

In attempting to understand D'Huisseau's condemnation by the Anjou synod, we must take two facts into consideration. The first is of a denominational nature. Though certain professors of the Saumur Academy desired to bring an end to the division of Christians, the majority of the pastors and elders in the Synod considered with repugnance the idea of reuniting with Catholicism. Certain reasons of a theological nature, but even more, perhaps, the trying pressures exerted upon Protestantism by the royal authorities and by the Roman church, explain their repulsion. On the whole, D'Huisseau was made to pay, not so much for the doctrinal errors imputed to him, but for the "ecumenical" aim of *La réunion du christianisme*. To this cause, and here we insist, another must be added that is of a purely personal nature. If D'Huisseau had not been the pet aversion of the Amyraldian clan, if he had not been exposed to the hostility of Gaussen and Beaujardin, the Anjou Synod would not have dared treat him as it did. In deposing and excommunicating the presumed author of *La réunion,* the pastors and elders of the Synod were, consciously or not, the accomplices of a well-directed plot.

Merciless toward D'Huisseau, the Anjou synod spared Tanneguy Lefèvre, who, in proper justice should have been condemned for having taken the initiative to publish *La réunion.* The Saumur philologist enjoyed such a reputation in the literary world that his co-religionists were unable to attack him. On the other hand, the Synod showed itself very severe toward Daniel Crespin, a student in theology who then assumed the functions of teacher in the Academy. For having corrected the proofs of *La réunion du Christianisme,* he was deprived of his functions. While D'Huisseau had accepted with an undeniable greatness the sentence that brutally interrupted his career, Crespin was unable to resist the need for loudly proclaiming his indignation. Breaking the anonymity with which the first defenders of D'Huisseau had surrounded themselves, he did not limit himself to the pleading his own cause in the *Apologie du Sieur D. Crespin où il fait voir les véritables motifs de sa condamnation au synode d'Anjou...* [42]. In the *Récit de ce qui s'est passé au Synode d'Anjou tenu a Saumur, l'an 1670, pour servir de factum à Monsieur D'Huisseau contre cette Compagnie* [43], he put his verve and acrimony to work for the excommunicated minister, victimized, according to him, by the pretentions of infallibility and by the tendency toward tyranny of his co-religionists.

Though, as we have just seen, the double condemnation of D'Huisseau was the result of Angevine Protestantism, the first literary offensive against him came from the Reformed circles of Paris. In 1670, indeed, Marc-Antoine de La Bastide[44], writer and elder of the Charenton Church, published in Saumur his *Remarques sur un livre intitulé la Réunion du christianisme...* [45]. This booklet was not exempt from a certain acrimony: it sought to have D'Huisseau condemned by the Catholics. But it revealed as well, on the doctrinal level, an undeniable perspicacity. The author felt that there was quite an audacity in attempting to use the Cartesian method in theology. "One can never say," he affirmed, "that it is possible to disengage oneself for a time from all that each communion of Christians possesses in particular and which separates it from the others" (pp. 14-15). He pointed out in addition that, in claiming to found the reconciliation of Christians on the Bible, thus excluding tradition, D'Huisseau forgot the reservations of Catholicism with respect to the principle of *sola Scriptura*. He showed, lastly, that in attempting to reduce Christianity to its fundamental doctrines, the Saumur minister retained a doctrinal nucleus capable of satisfying only the Arians and the Socinians. To conserve but the Apostle's Creed without sensing the necessity of the doctrine of the Trinity and that of the two natures, to reduce "the essence of religion to believing in the coming of the Son of God to the world with no further explanation" (p. 23), to presuppose that Scripture gives no clear teaching regarding the mode of incarnation, this was, for La Bastide, to open the door wide to numerous Christological heresies.

The *Remarques* did not remain unanswered. The same year of their publication there appeared, anonymously, *Remarques sur les remarques faites depuis peu sur le livre intitulé la Réunion du christianisme*[46]. This lampoon did not distinguish itself by its theological profundity. To the acrimony of La Bastide, it opposed the sharpest sarcasm, at the same time showing itself incapable of refuting the grievances of a doctrinal nature that the *Remarques* formulated against the book *La Réunion*. To the important reproach of Socinianism, for example, it simply opposed a sally: by holding that D'Huisseau was Socinian, La Bastide had simply imposed upon a few old women the idea that the Saumur pastor practiced "communication with the demons," that he was "well versed in the black science," that he had "for a library but the works of Agrippa" and that he found himself attending "the sabbath regularly each first Monday of the month"(p. 48).

The controversy aroused by *La Réunion du christianisme* could not reach any lower. It was the merit of the *Examen du livre de la Réunion. . . ou traité de la tolérance èn màtière de religion, et de la nature et de l'étendue des points fondamentaux. . .*[47] to restore discussion to the doctrinal level. This work was no more signed than had been the *Remarques* of La Bastide. But, without hesitation, the Protestants attributed it to Pierre Jurieu[48], then pastor in Mer. They were not wrong. In the *Examen* which inaugurated a polemical career of surprising fertility, the future adversary of Bossuet showed the cloven hoof: he betrayed himself by his harsh anger. Did he not there accuse D'Huisseau of not being in "the feelings of the Protestant Churches," but of nourishing sympathies for Catholocism (p. 312)! Did he not there insinuate with a wicked pleasure, as to burn the bridges before the one that he pursued with his anger, that the Roman Church could but condemn in turn the work censored by the Saumur Consistory and the Anjou Synod!

But it is not the personal attacks which, yet today, constitute the value of the *Examen*. It is rather, as we have already hinted, its strictly theological content. Jurieu does not disapprove of the intention of the book *La réunion*. It is good, he thinks, to work toward the reconciliation of all Christians. But it is necessary for this that the means employed be legitimate. Now those which *La réunion du christianisme* proposes are not such; rather, they are "criminal" (p. 9). To reunite believers, there are indeed but three possible paths. These are: 1) that of reformation where encounter takes place after having renounced one's respective errors; 2) that of silence where agreement takes place after having relegated all controversial subjects to the background; and 3) that of tolerance, which involves, after having come to agreement on certain general points, tolerating one another in all the other areas.

Remarking that neither the path of reformation, nor that of silence was followed in the book *La réunion*, Jurieu takes up a criticism, not of tolerance in general, but of that tolerance recommended by the condemned work. This tolerance would not in reality respect the fundamental articles. Favoring the development of all the "sects," of "all opinions and of all cults" (pp. 38-39), permitting the "monstrous assemblage of all of the most corrupt religions of the world under one selfsame communion" (p. 32), this would carry within it the seeds of Christianity's ruin. Invented by the devil, dear to the Arians as to the Socinians, this tolerance would be an offense to truth. By encouraging a spirit of indifference, it would be incapable of truly founding the union of Christians. Having thus attacked the notion of tolerance defended by the book *La réunion*, Jurieu proposes his own definition. By reason of an inexplicable inconsistency, he shows himself to be infinitely more broad minded than D'Huisseau. Thus, he cannot understand that one be excluded or excommunicated because of a difference of opinion on justification, good works, predestination, free will, grace and the efficacy of the sacraments.

After this attack against *La réunion du christianisme* on the chapter on tolerance, Jurieu gives himself over, in the *Examen*, to the criticism of the doctrine of the fundamental points defended by D'Huisseau. By holding that, "to avoid division and the sharing of opinions in the reading of Holy Scripture," we must stop at "the first most confused idea and the most general" (p. 211), *La réunion du christianisme* would propose a solution acceptable to all heretics. Even more precisely, in attempting to reduce to a small number the articles of faith, by setting aside the doctrines of the Trinity and of the two natures, it would follow a method of Socinian inspiration. It would hold "the former language and old style of all libertines" (p. 50) by advocating, following Descartes, methodical doubt. These objections formulated, Jurieu sets forth his own conceptions on the doctrine of the fundamental points. Once again, he contradicts himself by adopting an attitude that distinguishes itself in no way, other than by imperceptible shades of meaning, from that which he condemned in D'Huisseau.

The *Examen* provoked an immediate answer: the *Lettre écrite a Monsieur D'Huisseau au sujet de l'Examen du livre de la Réunion*[49[. The author of this anonymous epistle was a partisan of the pastor deposed by the Reformed authorities. While waiting for the letter to respond personally, he had taken up the pen with one sole goal: to prove that Jurieu was not, could not be, the author of the *Examen*. But who, then, would have composed this treatise? Gaussen, the *Lettre* affirmed without hesitation. The hypothesis is unlikely, but while sparing Jurieu, it constituted a dangerous threat for the dogmatician of the Saumur Academy. By depicting Gaussen as a theologian of advanced ideas and favorable to a more audacious "unionism" than that of the book *La reunion*, it sought to redirect toward him the blows that had just fallen upon D'Huisseau.

The *Lettre... au sujet de l'Examen...* was but a first riposte. Coming unexpectedly after that of La Bastide, the intervention of Jurieu compelled D'Huisseau to break the silence that he had proposed to keep until the meeting of a new assembly entrusted with the examination of his case. In 1671, he published a *Réponse... au livre intitulé Examen... de la Réunion du christianisme*[50]. This work, which often has the accents of a pathetic argument, did not defend only the anonymity and the opportuneness of the book *La Réunion*. After having attempted to prove its orthodoxy (it affirmed that neither the doctrine of the Trinity nor that of the divinity of Christ were excluded from it), D'Huisseau brought out again, not without pertinence, the contradictions of Jurieu. He asked, how can the author of the *Examen* reprove tolerance and yet consider it as applicable at the same time, in a provisional fashion to "essential and fundamental errors" (p. 141)? Is this not to "change the nature of things" according to one's good pleasure; is this not to change with "criminal" that which one considers an instant afterwards as "excellent, incomparable and divine" (p. 130)? In addition, D'Huisseau asked himself, how can Jurieu "rant" against the doctrine of the fundamental points exposed in *La Réunion du christianisme* and all the while not deviate in anything from it?

The criticisms that D'Huisseau addressed to Jurieu should not hide the fact that his concern for unity, in spite of his disappointments, had not been given up. His *Réponse* proposes an "ecumenical strategy" (if one may say so) even more elaborate than that of the book *La Réunion.* It recommends the abolition of denominational prejudices, prayer for unity, and finally the convocation of "special conferences and assemblies" where, grounding themselves upon Scripture, the participants would resolve questions of litigation and elaborate a common declaration of faith. But what to do if these efforts are not successful, if the conversations begun by the different Christian communions do not lead to their reconciliation? It is necessary to pursue them in spite of all, feels our author. "For it is too beautiful an enterprise to be turned aside by difficulties that one might encounter for a first, second and even a third time. The end of it is so good and looks so directly to the glory of God that one must not doubt that he will attend it at the end with his blessing" (p. 232).

The *Réponse* of D'Huisseau placed before Jurieu a number of important questions. The minister in Mer could not remain deaf to them, no more than he could feign to ignore the censure that the Saintonge Synod had carried out, in 1671, against certain propositions of the *Examen.* Thus, he had, published, the same year, the *Esclaircissement de quelques passages condamnés dans le livre de l'Examen de la Réunion du christianisme, avec quelques réflexions sur le dernier livre de Monsieur D'Huisseau* . . . [51]

This book expressed well the amazement with which Jurieu learned that the *Examen* had been suspected of Pelagianism, or at least semiPelagianism, by the Reformed of Saintonge. In order to exonerate himself, Jurieu there declared that his "opinions on grace" were "as rigorous as one must have" (p. 12); that he approved "the condemnation of the Arminians made by the Synod of Dort" (p. 14); in short, that he was ready to "sign with his blood" the truths of the La Rochelle Confession relative to salvation (p. 17). In holding in the *Examen* that one is free to "have differing opinions over the efficacy of grace, over the manner in which it excites the will and works together with free will, provided that one does not become Pelagian" (p. 146), he would not make the case, he affirms, that it is necessary to authorize "all heterodoxies which are below Pelagianism" (p. 37). In this argument *pro domo sua,* Jurieu accentuated a feature which had already appeared in the *Examen:* at the expense of the teaching of the Reformation, he minimized the debate on grace which is at the origin of the division between Catholics and Protestants. It is thus not surprising that the *Esclaircissement,* sent to the Synod of Saintonge, was unable to convince this synod of Jurieu's orthodoxy.

Full of the feeling that, by his explanations, he had succeeded in dissipating the concerns of his co-religionists of Saintonge, Jurieu published another work following the *Esclaircissement,* entitled *Quelques réflections sur le dernier livre de Monsieur D'Huisseau...* Concerned with refuting the answer of the latter, he sought to show that, in the *Examen,* he had sinned neither against "common sense" nor against "honesty." His notion of tolerance, he felt, presented no contradiction, and his manner of quoting the texts, contrary to the insinuations of his adversaries, was beyond all reproach. But the minister in Mer did not limit himself, to protestations of innocence. In order better to defend himself, he counterattacked vigourously. In maintaining that the fruits of *La réunion du christianisme* were poisonous, he intensified the accusation that he had raised in the *Examen.* By refusing the offer of reconciliation that D'Huisseau addressed to him at the end of his *Réponse,* he increased the misfortune of his excommunicated colleague. Overwhelmed by the infamy, D'Huisseau died in Saumur, one year later, without having experienced the public restoration that he desired so strongly.

French Protestantism in the 17th century experienced several controversies, of which certain ones, in particular that which was aroused by the *Brief traitté de la prédestination et de ses principales dependances,* [52] by Moise Amyraut, unleashed passions over several years. None of them, however, was, in its brevity, as harsh, as merciless, as that which was proviked by *La réunion du christianisme.* It was because, in the name of an "ecumenical" ideal to which the 20th-century reader is not insensitive, this work brought into question along with their doctrine, the very existence of the churches born of the Reformation. Animated by a desire for unity that confers on him an incontestable greatness, D'Huisseau, on the other hand, did not have the doctrinal understanding that would have permitted him to build his generous intentions upon solid foundations. In his defense, one must say that theological solidity was lacking in a great many of his contemporaries. The times were then not yet ready for the authentic dialogue in which, while intending to submit themselves to the imperative of unity, Catholics and Protestants are resolved to answer to all the requirements of truth.

NOTES

1. Paris, 1951
2. *Bossuet, historien du protestantisme,* Paris, 3rd. ed., 1909, p. 30
3. Published by René Péan; xviii + 208 pages.
4. The most important treatments of the D'Huisseau affair are the works of Frank Puaux, *Les Précurseurs français de la tolérance au xvii siècle,* Paris, 1881, pp. 75-81, and of René Voeltzel, *Vraie et fausse église selon les théologiens protestants francais du xvii siècle,* Paris, 1956, pp. 45-50. Though Puaux had the merit of bringing out D'Huisseau's importance, Voeltzel's merit was to bring out the main outlines of the 3rd part of *La réunion du christianisme,* the work which we are about to examine, and to establish the catalogue of the works published for or against D'Huisseau during the years 1670 and 1671. Neither Puaux nor Voeltzel recounted, however, the numerous vicissitudes of this case whose interest is highlighted in the article of Alfred Soman, "Arminianism in France: The D'Huisseau Incident", in *Journal of the History of Ideas,* 31, 1967, pp 597-600, to which I responded in my book, *L'affaire D'Huisseau,* Paris, 1969, and in an article in the *Bulletin de la Société de l'histoire du protestantisme français:* "D'Huisseau a-t-il plagié Arminius?" Paris, 1972, pp. 335-348.
5. Let us add to this fact that son of the elder of the Paris Church, D'Huisseau was born in that city and had done his theological studies in Sedan. Cf. Eugène et Emile Haag, *La France protestante,* Vol. 6, Paris, 1856, pp. 9-11; Célestin Port, *Dictionnaire historique, géographique et biographique de Maine-et-Loire,* Vol. 2, Paris and Angers, 1876, p. 375; and *Encyclopédie des sciences religieuses,* ed. by F. Lichtenberger, vol. 6, Paris, 1879, pp. 406-409.
6. David Crespin, *Récit de ce qui s'est passé au Synode d'Anjou,* 1671, pp. 44-45.
7. *Apologie pour le livre intitulé: La réunion du christianisme.* La Haye, 1670, p. 24.
8. *Lettres choisies,* vol. 3, 2nd ed., Amsterdam, 1730, p. 18.
9. We have knowledge of these proceedings through the excerpts given by Daniel Crespin, in his *Récit de ce qui s'est passé au Synode d'Anjou,* s. 1., 1671. Without Crespin's work, we would be in nearly total ignorance concerning the synod which was charged with examining the D'Huisseau case. Indeed, manuscript 431 of the *Bibliothèque de la Société de l'histôire du protestantisme francais,* in Paris, which contains the proceedings of the synods of the Anjou province, closes with the minutes of the Synod of Pruilly (1658).
10. Born in Caen, in 1615, within a catholic family, he was reared in the home of a clergyman uncle, before entering secondary school at La Flèche. After having assumed, thanks to the protection of Richelieu, the oversight of the Louvre printing office, he led over several years a somewhat rambling life (it was then that he publicly abjured the romanist religion) at which time he established himself as professor of Greek at Saumur, where he died in 1672. Cf. Eugène et Emile Haag, *La France protestante,* vol. 6, pp. 499-502.

11.   And not Louis Cappel the Younger, as A. Humbert writes (art. Jurieu, in *Dictionnaire de théologie catholique*, Vol. 8/2, col. 1996) and René Voeltzel (*op. cit.*, p. 45). Born in 1639, Jacques Cappel was called upon, at the age of 19, to succeed his father. Compelled to leave France after the revocation of the Edict of Nantes, he took refuge in England where he died in 1722. cf. *La France protestante*, 2nd ed., vol. 3. p. 736, and the article of E. Bertheau, in *Realencyklopädie für Theologie und Kirche*, 2nd ed. vol. 3, p. 139.

12.   Ousted by Jean-Robert Chouet when the chair of Philosophy became vacant at the Saumur Academy, in 1664, Pierre de Villemandy, born in 1636 or 1637, succeeded the Genevan in 1669, thanks to D'Huisseau's support, after having exercised the pastoral ministry in Saintonge. According to Bourchenin (cf. *Etude sur les Académies protestantes en France au XVIe et au XVIIe siècle*, Paris, 1882, p. 63), he withdrew himself in 1683, not because of his "advanced age" as the Haag brothers supposed (cf. *La France protestante*, vol. 9, p. 506), but in order to establish himself in the Netherlands. Having become regent of the Walloon college in Leyden, he died in that city in 1703 (cf. Elisabeth Labrousse, *Pierre Bayle*, vol. 2, p. 212, n. 105). On the philosophical position of Pierre de Villemandy, cf. chapter 5 of the Joseph Prost's work, *La philosophie à l'Académie protestante de Saumur (pp. 102-109)*

13.   *This letter, which was written immediately after the publication of the second part of vol. 3 of the Histoire de l'édit de Nantes*, (1695), is conserved along with two other missives relative to D'Huisseau addressed to Elie Benoist in the Antoine Court collection (vol. 48: *Recueil de mémoires etc., sur les protestants de France*, folios 21-26 vo) deposited at the Bibliotheque publique et universitaire de Genève and, in the form of a copy (sometimes faulty), at the Bibliothèque de la Société de L'Histoire du Protestantisme Francais, in Paris.

14.   Professor of theology at the Saumur Academy, Paul du Soul is virtually unknown. Native of Chinon, alumnus of the academies of Sedan and Geneva, he was seemingly rector of the Saumur academy in 1657 and in 1661 (cf. *La France protestante*, 2nd ed., vol. 5, p. 1072)

15.   Born in Romorantin in 1626, died in Carré near Orléans in 1685, Claude Pajon exercised the pastoral ministry in Marchenoir before being called as a professor at Saumur, in 1666. He resigned his functions, not in 1669 as Frank Puaux affirms (cf. *Encyclopédie des sciences religieuses*, vol. 10, p. 127) but in 1667 (cf. P. - Daniel Bourchenin, *Etude sur les Académies protestantes en France au XVIe et au XVIIe siècle*, p. 416) or in 1668 (cf. Eugène et Emile Haag, *La France protestante*, vol. 8, p. 67). Pajon gave up teaching so quickly because of the opposition that his semi-Arminian theology aroused in the Reformed churches. Leaving Saumur, he accepted the call of the Protestant parish of Orléans.

16.   Born in Vallorbe, in 1640 or 1641, of a French family established in the Vaud territory since the 16th century, Crespin considered himself as Swiss (cf. *Apologie du Sieur D. Crespin où il fait voir les véritables motifs de sa condamnation au Synode d'Anjou*, pp. 63, 72, 108 and 114). After having studied at Lausanne and Geneva, he came to Saumur, where, while assuming the task of regent of the fifth class, he prepared himself for the pastoral ministry. On Crespin, cf. *La France protestante*, 2nd ed., vol. 4, pp. 904-905, and, particularly, Henri Vuilleumier, *Histoire de l'Eglise réformée du pays de Vaud sous le régime bernois*, vol. 3, pp. 270-312 and 315-322.

17.   Pastor of the Reformed Church of Paris from 1666, he was considered as the "authorized man of French Protestantism" (*Encyclopédie des sciences religieuses*, vol. 3, p. 198).

18.   In the ungodliness, irreligion and atheism engendered by the division of Christians, D'Huisseau discovers the conditions favorable to the dawn of new religions. Thus, for him, Islam was able to appear only by "the favor of divers sects which were born formerly in the church" (p. 33).

19.   In his *Traité de l'église*, 1578; 2nd ed., La Rochelle, 1600, p. 23, D'Huisseau found himself in good company by utilizing this distinction.

20. On this question, cf. chapter 4 of Joseph Prost's work, *La philosophie à l'Académie protestante de Saumur* (pp. 69-101). It is surprising that Josef Bohatec, generally well-informed, would say nothing of the Cartesianism in Saumur in his thesis *Die Cartesianische Scholastik in der Philosophie und reformierten Dogmatik des 17. Jahrhunderts*, Leipzig, 1912. On the contrary, it is understandable that Ernst Bizer does not mention the school of Saumur, heterodox from a Reformed point of view, in his article, "Die reformierte Orthodoxie und der Cartesianismus" (in: *Zeitschrift für Theologie und Kirche*, Tübingen, 1958, pp. 306-372).

21. For, writes D'Huisseau, "otherwise we would give to man and to reason an authority which belong only to God alone and to his Word" (p. 154). As René Voeltzel has rightly brought out, this sentence permits us to "have reservations on D'Huisseau's Cartesianism or even his rationalism" (*op. cit.*, p. 48, n. 81)

22. The 17th century maps (cf. among others that of G. Sanson, *La terre et les isles Magellaniques*, Paris, 1668), situate the Magellan land at the southern extremity of South America, in a region that covers approximately Patagonia.

23. In his Ειρηνικον *sive de ratione pacis in religionis negotio inter Evangelicos constituendae consilium* (1662), Moses Amyraut already recommended this means.

24. Amyraut felt also in his Ειρηνικον that the success of the reuniting of Protestants depended on the princes. It is to them that he confided the responsibility to elicit "unionist" literature.

25. This affirmation came to be severely critized by the adversaries of D'Huisseau who will see in it the sign of a disturbing doctrinal uncertainty. The author of *La réunion du christianisme* appears indeed to furnish an echo, here, of a theological hesitation that he himself must have felt.

26. Cf. *La philosophie à l'Académie protestante de Saumur*, Paris, 1907, p. 100.

27. In writing this, we do not forget the distinction between doctrine (exposed in the confession of faith) and the discipline that D'Huisseau established in the foreword to the *Discipline*, dated April 30, 1666, and addressed to "Mssrs. Pastors of the Churches which are maintained in France under the favor of the edicts of the King" (cf. *Discipline des Eglises réformées de France*, Geneva, 1667, pp. 25-28). In virtue of this distinction, there must be consistency in doctrine, whereas discipline is always subject to revision. The "decisions" of doctrine are "distinctly carried by the Word of God," while discipline "is founded only upon a few general rules contained in the holy writings, as that of doing all things with order and decency" (p.31).

28. Cf. the Creed of the believer thrown into the Magellan (land) and the Creed where D'Huisseau expresses "the simplest and most naive doctrine of the Gospel."

29. Incidently, one might note that Reformed orthodoxy has never questioned this distinction. Cf. Heinrich Heppe, *Die Dogmatik der evangelisch-reformierten Kirche*, Neukirchen (Kreis Moers), 1935, pp. 34-36.

30. Cf. Johannes Dantine, *Die Prädestinationslehre bei Calvin und Beza*, Göttingen, 1965; "Das christologische Problem im Rahmen der Prädestinationslehre von Theodor Beza", in *Zeitschrift für Kirchengeschichte*, 1966, pp. 81-96; and "Les tabelles sur la doctrine de la predestination par Theodore de Bèze", in *Revue de théologie et de philosophie*, Lausanne, 1966, pp. 365-377.

31. It has often been attempted to see Moïse Amyraut as the most famous among them. Without pretending to take up the delicate problem of knowing whether or not the "hypothetical universalism" of the theologian is an "attenuated, but original form" of Arminianism (Emile-G. Léonard, *Histoire générale du protestantisme*, vol. 2, p. 336), we feel with Alexander Schweizer (cf. *Die protestantischen Centraldogmen*, vol. 2, Zürich, 1856, p. 297), Francois Laplanche (cf. *Orthodoxie et prédication. L'oeuvre d'Amyraut et la*

querelle de la grâce universelle, p. 270) and Brian G. Armstrong (cf. *Calvinism and the Amyraut Heresy*, p. 269) that there is a great difference between Amyraut's system and the Arminian doctrine.

32. *Lettres choisies*, vol. 3, 2nd ed., Amsterdam, 1730, p. 18.

33. *Histoire de l'édit de Nantes*, vol. 3/2, Delft, 1695, p. 145.

34. Born in Nîmes, he was in 1661 professor of logic and metaphysics, and from 1664 to his death (1675) professor of theology at the Saumur Academy. Cf. Eugène and Emile Haag, *La France protestante*, vol. 5, pp. 235-236, and Célestin Port, *Dictionnaire historique, géographique et biographique de Maine-et-Loire*, vol. 2, Paris and Angers, 1876, p. 238.

35. Beaujardin is, so to speak, unknown. One knows only that he exercised the pastoral ministry during forty years in Saumur and that, as an old man, he abjured in La Rochelle. Cf. Eugène and Emile Haag, *La France protestante*, 2nd ed., vol. 2, p. 21-22.

36. *Apologie pour le livre intitulé la Réunion du christianisme et pour celuy qui en a esté soupçonné l'autheur a Saumur*, La Haye, 1670, p. 212

37. Daniel Crespin, *Récit de ce qui s'est passé au Synode d'Anjou tenu à Saumur, l'an 1670, pour servir de factum a Monsieur D'Huisseau contre cette compagnie*, s. 1., 1671, p. 126.

38. François de Haumont was Amyraut's son-in-law.

39. No indication of place, 1670, 107 pages.

40. Published by Rogier Comans, La Haye, 1670, 224 pages.

41. No indication of place, 1670, 102 pages.

42. No indication of place, 1671, 115 plus 20 pages

43. No indication of place, 1671, xxii plus 183 pages.

44. Born in Millau towards 1624, La Bastide was expelled from France in 1687. He retired to England and died in London in 1704. Cf. Eugène and Emile Haag, *La France protestante*, vol. 6, pp. 151-152.

45. Published by René Péan, Saumur, 67 pages.

46. No indication of place, 73 pages.

47. Neither indication of place (=Orléans), nor publisher's name (=Rousselet), xv plus 424 pages.

48. Born in Mer in 1673, Jurieu studied in Saumur and in Sedan, before visiting the Universities of Holland and England, After having exercised the pastoral ministry in Mer, he was appointed as professor at the Academy of Saumur. When this Academy was closed in 1681, he took the functions of professor at the theological School of Rotterdam. He died there in 1713. Cf. Eugène and Emile Haag, *La France Protestante*, vol. 6, pp. 104-113; and Frederik Reinier Jacob Knetsch, *Pierre Jurieu, theoloog en politikus der refuge*, Kampen, 1967; *Encyclopédie des sciences religieuses*, vol. 7, pp. 551-559).

49. The copy of this booklet (56 pages) which we have utilized having lost its title page, we are unable to indicate either the place nor the date of its publication. It is in any case anterior to the *Reponse de Monsieur D'Huisseau au livre intitulé Examen du livre de la Réunion du christianisme*, published in 1671.

50. Without publisher's name, 1671, Paris, 247 pages.

51. Without publisher's name, Sedan, 1671, 149 pages.

52. Published in 1634, the *Brief traitté de la prédestination* provoked a controversy which lasted thirty years until the death of Amyraut in 1664.